SONIA DUCIE MAR. Dip.CSN. AIN

Sonia Ducie is a professional numerologist. She has written 11 numerology books, and has been teaching, and giving consultations to businesses and individuals for more than 15 years. Sonia has also practised reflexology for 17 years. Her previous background is journalism and public relations.

By the same author

Power Pendants In A Box
Do It Yourself Numerology
Numerology Gem
Directions For Life – Numerology
Sonia Ducie's Numerology Secrets
The Lucky Numbers Oracle
Complete Illustrated Guide To Numerology
Numerology: Your Personal Guide For Life
Numerology: Your Love & Relationship Guide
The Principles Of Numerology
The Self Help Reflexology Handbook

NUMEROLOGY
Your Personal Guide for Life

SONIA DUCIE

WATKINS PUBLISHING
LONDON

Distributed in the USA and Canada by Sterling Publishing Co., Inc.
387 Park Avenue South, New York, NY 10016

This edition published in the UK and USA 2009 by
Watkins Publishing, Sixth Floor, Castle House,
75–76 Wells Street, London W1T 3QH

First published in 1999 by Element Books Limited

Text Copyright © Sonia Ducie 1999, 2009

1 3 5 7 9 10 8 6 4 2

Additional material typeset by Dorchester Typesetting Group

Printed and bound in Great Britain

Library of Congress Cataloging-in-Publication Data Available

ISBN: 978-1-906787-10-3

www.watkinspublishing.co.uk

For information about custom editions, special sales, premium and
corporate purchases, please contact Sterling Special Sales
Department at 800-805-5489 or specialsales@sterlingpub.com.

Thank you to Claudine Aegerter and
all at AIN – it's the beginning!

CONTENTS

INTRODUCTION

CHAPTER 1

PERSONAL YEARS AND YOUR HEALTH   21

CHAPTER 2

PERSONAL YEARS AND YOUR CAREER   69

INTRODUCTION

WHAT IS NUMEROLOGY

NUMEROLOGY is a science, a psychology and a philosophy. It is a science because it is a method for you to find your way around in an objective way, a psychology, because it offers you information about your psychological patterns of behaviour, and it is a philosophy or a way of life too. It is a wonderful and practical tool which enables you to understand more about yourself and the world you live in. Numerology can take you to great depths of profound knowledge and understanding about your life by applying a powerful key which helps to unlock your sub-conscious mind. It therefore helps to reveal more information about the 'real' you and hidden aspects contained within your chart.

There are many different methods of numerology applied in many cultures around the world today – indeed numbers began when time began – having launched itself out of the eternal zero. Many ancient practices are still used today. Divination is mainly used for prediction, Esoteric Numerology highlights concepts behind numbers to reveal the inner mysteries of life and the universe; the Kabbalah, or the application of numerology within names, is also used;

and Pythagorian Numerology remains one of the most popular methods of numerology used in the West today.

Pythagoras was passionate about his sciences, particularly numbers, and in addition to being a brilliant mathematician and philosopher he was also an aspiring numerologist. He developed his own methods of training the intuition with numerology at his School of Mysteries in ancient Greece around 600 BC. Pythagoras developed the cycles 1 to 9. He believed numbers to be 'the essence of all life'. This book has a Pythagorian flavour, but it is strongly influenced by my training in Esoteric Numerology and also encompasses my observations of numbers in the ever-changing world in which we live.

Numbers are not solid objects but are moving energies or vibrations, and each number contains the potential for light or positive experiences (connection) and the dark shadow side or negative experiences (separation) within them. These vibrations influence your life and each number carries with it the potential for many, many different experiences. In numerology each number highlights qualities, both strengths and challenges, which are carried within its potential. Each number also contains spiritual, mental, emotional and physical elements.

From your date of birth to the time of your death numbers influence your every move. Numbers in money, your office, your home, your names, and so on, all add up to give an overall influence over your life every minute of the day. However, with numerology numbers are not valued (as with money) but simply understood.

Numerology, along with being a useful and practical guide that can help you with day-to-day situations in your life, is also a wonderful personal development tool because it offers you self-awareness, which can in itself encourage self-responsibility and choice. It is tremendous fun to use and it's exciting when you realize why things are occurring in your life simply by observing the numbers around you. Numerology can help you to live in the moment and make the most out of your life by being aware of the energies that are available to you. It can also help you to develop your '6th sense' and to learn to trust your instincts and your intuition about the jewels of information which each number is revealing to you.

Your date of birth and the names on your birth certificate carry the most significance and have the most influence over your life. This is because the exact time and date on which you were born brings with it an alignment of energies which are available for you to 'work with' in your lifetime. The numbers in your date of birth provide you with your maximum potential in life. Your names are karmically given to you by your parents or guardians and these energies can help you to learn the lessons that you need to learn. Each letter in your name is translated into numbers by applying it to the alphabet, A = 1, B = 2, and so on . . .

Your date of birth reveals two of the most significant numbers influencing your life – your Personality Number and your Life Path Number. Your Personality Number is found by adding up the day of the month on which you were born, and this gives your psychological pattern of behaviour. If you wish to find out more about your personality number, please see my book *Do It Yourself Numerology*. Your Life Path Number is found by adding up your whole date of birth, and this reveals the bigger picture or your direction or purpose in life, and it also contains deeper soul elements within it as well.

Sometimes the Personality and Life Path Numbers conflict with each other and you may find conflict with where you fit into the bigger picture and what it is you *want* to do with your life. For example, your Personality Number may be a 2 and your career may be in nursing, but your Life Path Number may be an 8, which means you may have a good head for business. Perhaps you feel conflict about your career, and it may seem that you are being pulled in two different directions. Of course you can compromise and follow both careers but at different times in your week or life. My book *Numerology: Your Love and Relationship Guide* explains more about this relationship and also about your compatibility with others in your life.

The next most important number which influences your life is your Karma Number, which is found by adding up all the names on your birth certificate (or the full names by which you were first known). This number brings with it gifts and karmic influences over your life. Karma is the law of reward and retribution; everything you do in the past comes back to you; your thoughts and your actions. This number reveals information about your past lives too.

Working out your Personality, Life Path and Karma Numbers is essential so that you can understand more about the kinds of experiences which may occur during your Personal Year cycles as explained in this book. This is because when any of these three numbers come up on your Personal Year cycles they play a significant role in your life. When you first look at the fascinating world of numerology all these numbers may seem mesmerizing, but this book will show you clearly how to work out all the major numbers in your chart (*see* Working Out Your Personal Numbers on page 11). Once you have calculated your numbers, relax and let your intuition guide you along with the information given in these pages.

NUMEROLOGY CYCLES AND YOUR PERSONAL YEARS

In life timing is everything and although you may think that you are in control of your life actually there is always a bigger power or force guiding it. Indeed, the Universal Year Numbers (explained later in this chapter) give you some indication of the collective energies that influence everyone's lives. Cycles are the foundation of life and the more you become aware of how these cycles are influencing you the more it can help you to make the most of your life. Your body has its own cycles and rhythms. In terms of your health for example, during a 3 cycle you may find that perhaps you get a muscular injury which forces you to slow down the pace of your life for a while. A 3 quality can influence you to be excessively active and perhaps your body is giving you just what you need by getting you to relax. All illness ultimately brings you back to your true self (your soul) and by being aware of each cycle the numbers can help to teach you exactly what you need to learn.

Life is a series of patterns or cycles and in numerology these evolve and transform in cycles of between 1 to 9. A precis of these cycles is sketched on page 16 and they are explored in depth later on. Any number over 9 can be added up to form one of these simple yet powerful vibrations. Through the observation of number patterns or cycles you can find out about your health, your relationships, your career and about any situation you may find yourself in. By observing your chart you may understand why for example, you may wish to start a new relationship in a 9 or 1 year cycle, leave a job in a 5 year, and so on . . . These Personal Year Numbers bring awareness, so that you can make the most of the energies which are available to you right now, in order to help you lead a happier, healthier and more successful life.

These number cycles are found in your date of birth and your names, but in addition there are other significant cycles which are governing your life. These are called your Personal Year cycles, which run in 9 year cycles (from 1 to 9). Your Personal Year cycles run from one birthday to the next and they are very important because they influence the kind of experiences you may have during each specific year. For example if your Personal Year Number is a 2 then decision-making is one aspect of your life which may be highlighted this year. Naturally most people make decisions (whether small or a large) on a daily basis, but particularly when a 2 is influencing your life then being aware of the importance of decision-making may be very helpful.

The first 6 years of your Personal Year cycles are full of many experiences which in your 7th Personal Year can be brought together in some way. For example, you may travel around the world for 6 years and in the 7th year you may write a book about your travels which would bring together all your previous 6 years of experiences. Your 8th year influences birth and rebirth, therefore summing up the experiences you have learned in the last 7 Personal Years of your cycle. An 8 also influences karma, and you may feel a strong need to re-evaluate in an 8 year, as situations and people from the past revisit your life. The 9 Personal Year influences the freedom to let go and transform situations in your life.

Although one 9th of the world is sharing the same Personal Year Number as you, no two people experience the same situations in their life because their dates of birth and names are all different. However, you are working with similar issues. For example, you may be married or single but if you are in a 7 Personal Year then working on one of its aspects – the quality of 'trust' – is a universal lesson.

As with all the numbers in your chart, your Personal Year Numbers bring with them the potential for positive or negative experiences. Negative qualities are in effect challenges for you to work on which can be transformed into positive qualities or attributes, or experiences which can be turned around into positive learning lessons. For example, if your Personal Year Number is a 1 and you may sometimes be unfocused (one of its qualities), then you may consciously choose to work on this during your 1 Personal Year and develop a steadier ability to focus. The ability to focus may influence your whole life in a positive way. This is what is called transforming a pattern.

Life is for learning and each number cycle teaches you about different aspects of yourself and influences you in different ways. Indeed, although all the numbers 1 to 9 carry with them many potential experiences, the fact that your age changes every time you go through the same cycles 1 to 9 means you can experience things very differently. For example, if you are in a Personal Year 5 and you are aged 23, by the time you reach your next 5 Personal Year (9 years later) when you are aged 32 then your outlook on life as a result of your increased maturity means that you can interpret experiences differently.

Each time you go through a 5 Personal Year you will consciously, or subconsciously, remember previous times when you were influenced by that Personal Year vibration and what events happened to you or what lessons you were learning then. For example, perhaps when you were aged 16 you moved house and were very restless and unsettled. In your current 5 Personal Year you may feel restless again and even feel like moving home again. But by recognizing this is what you did in your last 5 cycle you can make your choices based on your current circumstances and not because you are being influenced by your past. Indeed it may be your choice to work on structuring your life systematically in a 5 Personal Year to help you to feel even more secure in your life.

Perhaps you experienced a big trauma in a 4 Personal Year and 9 years later when that number 4 is influencing your life again you may remember the trauma vividly. However, reliving the memory of that trauma in that year even for a moment may actually help you to recognize that the specific event was a thing of the past, and may enable you to let it go. Sometimes, people who have memory lapses as a result of trauma may actually consciously reconnect with that trauma when they find themselves influenced by that same number vibration again. In some cases this may help them to unblock the past and move on.

Each time you come through a 9 cycle and begin a fresh 9 Personal Year you do not revisit the exact place you were in before because you will have grown wiser from some of the experiences you have been through. Life and numbers show you the lessons you need to learn, and life is about learning and relearning, and sometimes it seems like you take one step forward and two steps back. For example, you may revisit old situations or recurring patterns which become particularly intense during specific Personal Year cycles; history repeats itself sometimes. You may learn lessons about other problems or situations which may disappear completely from your life or they may still occur but make little impact upon your life.

As you go through life's training ground no experience is ever lost, and what you have learned today you carry with you into tomorrow. So for example, within your career, if you were a lawyer at the age of thirty and a graphic artist at the age of thirty-nine, then you can use your abilities to negotiate (which you learned about whilst being a lawyer) to work out fair contracts with your clients now. Experiences you have learned in the past contribute to who you are right now, and by being yourself now you can influence all the future cycles you may go through. Being aware of your Personal Year cycles can help you learn how to work *with* the changes which occur during each cycle of your life.

UNIVERSAL OR COLLECTIVE YEAR NUMBERS

Everyone and everything on this earth is a part of nature and therefore, as seen in numerology, no matter what the influence of your personal cycles may be, the greater cycles of life ultimately have the final say. For example, if you are in a 4 Personal Year and feeling physically secure, if there is snow and ice on the ground then each step you make may be precarious. Weather conditions are a cyclical part of nature which play a huge role in your life. Some of the larger cycles which influence you are birth and death, the seasons, the weeks in the year, the days in the week, night and day, and so on. Economic, social and political trends are also influenced by the Universal Year Number

In numerology, you can learn more about these larger cycles by working out the Universal Year Number, which can give you information about collective or universal influences each appropriate year. To do this you simply add up the year numbers together. So for example, if you would like to find out about the general trends for the year 2009 then add up $2 + 0 + 0 + 9 = 11$. $1 + 1 = 2$. Therefore

2 is the Universal Year cycle which will influence the whole world in the year 2009. This number is very potent and in terms of world history by looking back (in the year 2009) to the last time the world was in a 2 year cycle (in 2000) you can observe what lessons or experiences the world was going through then and see if the world has learned these lessons. Perhaps the same weather patterns were repeated during that year, and so on. 2018 will be a new 2 cycle.

If your Personal Year Number is the same as the Universal Year Number this can mean your potential, for both positive and challenging experiences, may be more intense. For example, if the world is experiencing a spiritual upsurge in the year 2014 (adds up to a 7) and your Personal Year Number is a 7 too then you may intensely develop the spiritual aspects in your life, or deepen your spiritual connection with yourself or others. Perhaps you experience the challenging aspects of the 7 too. When both the Universal and your Personal Year Numbers are in sync then you may feel particularly aligned with nature – or at one. However, some people are more in tune and therefore influenced by the collective Universal Year cycles than their own, and if this is the case with you then you may be strongly atuned to the bigger picture in life too. But even when you only identify with your own Personal Year cycles then, subconsciously, nature is still influencing every moment of your life.

Many people in the world are also influenced by the same Personal Year Number vibrations as you at any given time, and therefore you are always collectively working with others in the world.

NUMEROLOGY: YOUR GUIDE FOR LIFE

You do not need to be a brilliant mathematician like Pythagoras to practise or incorporate numerology into your life, but you do need to be able to perform simple additions and subtractions. You also need to be able to open your mind fully and perhaps to allow yourself to get drunk on the wisdom and truth contained within these simple digits.

WORKING OUT YOUR PERSONAL NUMBERS

In order for you to make the most out of the knowledge in this book it is essential for you to be able to work out the most important numbers in your chart. These are your Personality Number, your Life Path Number, your Karma or Wisdom Number, and of course your Personal Year Number.

In addition, you can learn how to work out your Personal Month, Personal Week and even your Personal Day numbers so that you can become even more acutely aware of the natural cycles influencing your life. These numbers also play a part in the kind of experiences that may occur, but the Personal Year Number is the most powerful. However, the Universal Year Number has a large say over your life too. But, your Personal Year cycle will give you experiences and qualities for you to work with during each specific year, whatever is going on universally.

Calculating Your Personality Number

Your Personality Number contains your potential psychological patterns of behaviour. To find this number simply add up the numbers in the day of the month on which you were born.

Example: Sarah Jane Smith born 27th November
27 is the day in the month on which Sarah was born. To find a digit between 1 and 9 simply add the compound digits together. That is $2 + 7 = 9$. Therefore Sarah's Personality Number is 9.

Calculating Your Life Path Number

Your Life Path Number gives you information about where you fit into the bigger picture in life and gives you your potential direction in life. It also contains soul elements too. Find your Life Path Number by simply adding up all the numbers in your date of birth.

Example: Sarah Jane Smith was born 27th November 1984

Add up the day and month of birth, $27 + 11 = 38$
Add up the year of birth $1984 = 1 + 9 + 8 + 4 = 22$
Add up $38 + 22 = 60$
To find a single digit between 1 and 9 add $6 + 0 = 6$
Therefore Sarah's Life Path Number is a 6

Calculating Your Karma Or Wisdom Number

Your Karma Number (often described as a Wisdom Number because it contains potential gifts from your past experiences), gives you information about your past lives and potential additional lessons for you to learn in this life-time. For your Karma Number simply translate all the letters in the full name on your birth certificate (or the first names by which you were first known), and add them up.

Example: Sarah Jane Smith

Firstly translate the letters into numbers from the key below:

KEY TO THE ALPHABET

1	A	J	S
2	B	K	T
3	C	L	U
4	D	M	V
5	E	N	W
6	F	0	X
7	G	P	Y
8	H	Q	7
9	I	R	

Therefore S = 1, A = 1, R = 9, and so on. Carry on until you have numbers for all her names.

Sarah Jane Smith
11918 1155 14928 = 56

Add up 5 + 6 = 11
Add 1 + 1 = 2
Therefore Sarah's Karma Number is a 2

Working Out Your Personal Year Cycles

Your Personal Year Number runs from one birthday to the next and influences the kind of experiences which may occur during that year.

Example: Sarah Jane Smith born 27.11.1984 day.month.year) Today's date 24th June 2009

Step 1

Add up the year of your last birthday. Sarah's last birthday
was in 2008 (because she has not yet had her birthday this
year). That is $2 + 8 = 10, 1 + 0 = 1$.

Step 2

Add up your day and month of birth. Sarah's day and
month of birth is 27th November, so add $27 + 11 = 38$,
$3 + 8 = 11, 1 + 1 = 2$.

Step 3

Now add the two final numbers in Step 1 and 2. That is
$1 + 2 = 3$. Therefore from November 2008 to November
2009 Sarah's Personal Year Number is a 3. This will change
in November 2009 when her Personal Year Number will
be a 4, and so on. When Sarah reaches her birthday in
2015 she will start a new 9 year cycle and will be
influenced by a 1 Personal Year again.

Calculating Your Personal Month, Week and Day Numbers

Your Personal Month, Week and Day Numbers give you
influences which, because they are governed overall by
your Personal Year Number are less potent, but nonetheless
important.

To calculate your Personal Month number add your
Personal Year Number to the current month.

Example: Sarah Jane Smith's Personal Year Number is currently a 3 (see above), and today's date is 24th June 2009.

Add the Personal Year Number 3 to the current month
(June) 6, so $3 + 6 = 9$. Therefore Sarah's Personal Month
Number this month of June is a 9. In July it will be a 1,
and so on . . .

To calculate your Personal Week Number simply add your Personal Year Number to the current week number.

Example: Sarah Jane Smith's Personal Year Number is a 3. Today's date is the 24th June 2009.

Add Sarah's Personal Year Number 3 to the current week number (on 24th June) week 25 = 3 + 25 = 28, 2 + 8 = 10, 1 + 0 = 1. So Sarah's Personal Week Number is a 1.

Finally to work out your Personal Day Number simply add the current day in the month to your Personal Month Number.

Example: Sarah Jane Smith's Personal Month Number is a 9. Today's date is the 24th June 2009.

Add Sarah's Personal Month Number 9 to the current day in the month 24. 9 + 24 = 33, 3 + 3 = 6. Therefore on today's date, 24th June 2009, Sarah's Personal Day Number is a 6.

Calculating the Universal Year Number

This is a number which changes every year, and influences the major trends and cycles of events within the whole world. As you are a part of the world this number has a huge significance in your life. To work out this number simply add up the numbers contained within the appropriate year.

Examples: 2010 = 2 + 0 + 1 + 0 = 3, or Universal Year 3
2011 = 2 + 0 + 1 + 1 = 4, or Universal Year 4
2012 = 2 + 0 + 1 + 2 = 5, or Universal Year 5
and so on.

Personal Cycles 1 to 9

Personal Year cycles are also relevant to your Personal Month, Week and Day cycles. So, for example, if your Personal Year, Month, Week or Day Number is a 7 you will still be influenced by this number during the appropriate cycle.

However there are simple generalizations with the numbers which are easy to apply and understand. The following numbers can also be applied to the Universal Year Number too:

CYCLES
1 = New direction
2 = Balance
3 = Expansion
4 = Consolidation
5 = Changes
6 = Wholeness
7 = Completion
8 = Karma
9 = Transformation

Numbers in Your Life

Once you start to become aware of the regular and natural cycles of 1 to 9 and how they influence your life you can learn to make the most out of every situation that comes your way.

THE PERSONAL YEAR CYCLES 1 TO 9

It usually takes a while to work your way around a subject but with numerology you are given instant access to information whether you have learned anything about the qualities contained within the numbers or not. This is because numbers speak to your subconscious mind and reveal to you hidden information via your intuition and mind. Of course it is very useful to have guidelines to what each number potentially means; when you are learning to ride a bike you need some lessons. And like learning to read a road map you usually get to know the big roads first and all the little roads (the fine tuning) later on. This book focuses on one area or one route – your Personal Year cycles – where you can find out more about yourself through self-awareness, personal growth, understanding and wisdom.

When you are learning and finding out about this wonderful tool it's helpful to relax and to enjoy the numbers, and allow them simply to fall into place. Numerology is fascinating, and usually the more you learn, the more you want to know. It is a never-ending subject because numbers are mirrors of life and you are continually changing and learning!

In order to make the most out of this book, it is helpful to be aware that numbers are moving energies and each number contains a little of the number before and after it in sequence, because one number flows into the next. This is particularly so at the time of your birthday when your Personal Year Number changes from one number to the next. This means, for example, if you are in a 7 Personal Year then you are also influenced to some degree by the energies of the 6 and 8 Personal Year Numbers too. Around the

time of your birthday the previous number 6 will be particularly mingled with your 7 Personal Year energies, and at
the time of your birthday in your Personal Year, the 7 year
energy will strongly be linking together with the experiences and qualities of the 8 too. However, the actual
Personal Year Number you are in, always bears the strongest
influence over your life.

When you enter a Personal Year you do not become
that number, indeed you are not a number, numbers
influence you. But you simply find yourself being aware of
different qualities, or you may find yourself focusing on
different things, and so on, as a result of the Personal
Year vibration.

When you read about the kinds of potential experiences contained within each appropriate Personal Year
Number in this book, you may identify with some of its
qualities and experiences but not with others. This is
because they are contained within the number's potential,
and therefore you may only experience a few of its experiences, qualities or lessons in this lifetime. Perhaps you may
also learn about some qualities, experiences or lessons
from each number later on in your life, when you are
influenced by that Personal Year Number again. For
example, if you read that during a 4 Personal Year the
potential is that you take a cookery course or learn account-
ancy then you may think 'this is not for me' but they may be
things you actually choose to do later on in your life, or you
may not do it at all.

You can react differently each time you are influenced by
a Personal Year vibration as a result of the Universal Year
Number. This is a greater cycle which affects everyone collectively, and is the Universal Year you are experiencing
collectively, like 2011 which adds up to a 4, and so on. You

are also influenced by your Personality, Life Path and Karma Numbers which all interact differently during each Personal Year cycle, and on the spiritual, mental, emotional and physical levels too.

Sometimes your Personality, Life Path or Karma Number aligns with your Personal Year Number, and these can be extra special times of learning. Indeed positive lessons and challenges can both be highlighted and intensified during that specific year (from birthday to birthday). For example, if your Life Path Number is a 3 and you are influenced by a 3 Personal Year then it can make issues connected with this number (like self-expression) more potent during that year. Alternatively if you have one number which is strongly missing from your chart (for example a number 2) and you enter a 2 Personal Year then this may help to bring out some of its qualities from within you.

Numbers repeat themselves, that is life, and with each turn of the spiral they release more information that can help you with your life. You will feel more comfortable with some numbers or energies than with others, but all your experiences can teach you something about yourself.

This book enables you to learn about your personal rhythms and cycles, and by being clear with yourself about the lessons and your experiences in life, it can help you to lead a happier and even a more successful life. Indeed 'energy follows thought', which means whatever you give your mind or thoughts to can potentially be created, so being positive during each cycle can really help. This book is a guide for life, because each time you go through a 1 to 9 cycle it can bring you new awareness.

Have fun!

1

PERSONAL YEARS AND YOUR HEALTH

HEALTH means different things to different people. It may conjure up a vision of healthy foods, exercise, sex, or a vision of prayer and stillness. Perhaps you envisage a perfectly toned body or a shiny skin or clear and bright eyes? However, good health is actually the ability to balance the mind, body and spirit and this can be extremely difficult to do at times. For example, perhaps you have a strong and robust physical body, a strong and positive mind, but you are very emotional which means you feel vulnerable and hypersensitive some of the time. There are four levels to the body: physical, emotional, mental and spiritual, and when even one of these levels is out of sync it can affect your whole health.

When you become ill or your health goes out of balance, even for a short time, it is your inner self telling you that some issues in your life need to be looked at. Being ill can sometimes be a wonderful learning opportunity and a positive experience which can teach you more about yourself. For example, when someone has a heart-attack and they change their lifestyle or attitude towards life, it can sometimes help to prolong their life. Therefore illness is another part of the balancing process.

All life is interconnected and your health is also influenced by your external environment (which mirrors the internal environment in which you live). So for example, if you have moved house and everyone around you is moaning and very negative about the new home, you may get sick – with flu for instance – to release negative thought forms (toxins) which have built up.

In this chapter you can see general health trends are contained within the potential for each Personal Year cycle.

PERSONAL YEAR
1

When you are influenced by a 1 Personal Year then you are at the beginning of a whole new 9 year cycle. This is exciting and in terms of your health it may inspire you to 'clean out the cupboards' and start again. This may mean that if you have been neglecting your health during the last 9 years you may like to work out new goals and set yourself new targets to work towards this coming year. Indeed, you may like to set yourself new trends for the next 9 year cycle as well.

This may mean studying your diet to see ways in which you can improve your health; perhaps by adding extra protein, carbohydrates or fats to your diet or cutting down on them, or drinking more water and so on . . . As this is a time for fresh beginnings perhaps you may decide to go the whole hog and consult a professional nutritionalist or naturopath who can give you solid advice about what diet is best suited to you.

In a 1 Personal Year you may decide to take up some physical exercise to help keep you fit and healthy. The 1 energy brings in the potential for you to work to build up your physical stamina in some way. Perhaps you choose to do this by taking up a really physical exercise like jogging, running (perhaps you may even decide to run a marathon), rowing, cycling, aerobics, and so on.

Of course you don't need to do everything straight away or to become fit overnight, although with this 1 energy influencing you it may feel like it at times. This is because a 1 is a very dynamic energy and with this influence you are likely to feel the need to dive into things and to go for goals one hundred per cent. This can be marvellous, particularly if after only one week of giving up smoking or jogging around the block (for example), you notice your skin glowing a little brighter. Encouragement may also come from your friends or lover telling you how much more positive you are and so on.

The 1 also influences the mind, and with a 1 Personal Year you may notice that your capacity to deal with life's stresses decreases at times. This is because the 1 energy emphasizes thinking, and too much mental over-stimulation can overload you, or in extreme cases may lead to some kind of mental breakdown.

However, if you are normally someone who jumps into things without thinking, this 1 energy can help you bring more mental focus into your life. For example, if you have been day-dreaming about what it is like to be slimmer and you throw yourself into a crash diet, then yes you may lose weight very quickly, but you may be physically weakened as a result. By thinking about what the consequences of a crash diet may be you may save yourself more mental anguish and worry about a possible need to gain weight again to get your stamina back after an unsuitable diet.

With the 1 influencing you this Personal Year learning how to keep your mind healthy by focusing on the positive side of life can really help. Physical exercise can help to bring in positive energy because it helps to release any pent-up emotions, mental worries, stresses, and toxins too. However, learning some new mental activity can also help to keep your mind healthy, which can influence your whole body. For example, you may decide to take up chess, read more books or literature, particularly about subjects which you enjoy, which can all help to keep your mind focused in a positive way.

During this 1 Personal Year you can also learn to train your mind to focus on your goals, or to focus on other areas which may be out of balance in your life. For example, perhaps you have been neglecting your health, and so on. When your mind is trained to focus it means that physical energy seems to pour into you out of nowhere and you can sometimes go on and on. This is because when your mind is in charge it tells your body what to do: 'No, you can't get a cold at the moment, you've got too much to do . . . Yes, you can keep exercising another half-hour, you've got to get fit!' and so on. Training your mind to focus means that you can sometimes go on with little sleep, although the body needs to rest to stay healthy too.

With the 1 energy influencing your health during this Personal Year cycle it can mean that you seem able to focus on things more easily than in the other Personal Year cycles (2 to 9). If you know that you need to get healthy then taking advantage of the focus that is potentially available to you this year may really help.

In a year of new beginnings, if you take up many of the new opportunities that may come your way, then you may become ill. Failing to recognize the warning signs when your body feels depleted of energy or has raised stress levels may leave you run down. However, once you do recognize these signs you can quickly focus to get back on track.

Marjorie is a schoolteacher and has a Life Path Number 1, and at the beginning of 2008 she was also in a 1 Personal Year which intensified the energies of this number. She is naturally very ambitious and during that year she found that she took on a project which was too demanding and she became so tired that she just couldn't think. Luckily she took some time off to rest and soon regained her strength and her direction.

25

The number 1 highlights new direction and sometimes arriving in your new 9 year cycle can feel threatening, as you may not know which route to take in your life. When you have a lack of direction your whole body can go out of balance as there is no mental focus. However, if you do get ill, then this can give you the space to withdraw and to work out exactly what it is you need to do next. As you withdraw into your mind you may find a whole new direction appears, and the more you focus positively on the next step, the more energy you have to move forward. Energy follows thought and positive thoughts can help you to stay healthy and happy.

Another reason you may become ill in a 1 Personal Year is when life seems to be running away with you, and you feel as though you have no say over your life. Perhaps you have a temporary illness because you feel you are being forced to do something, or to avoid dealing with a situation head on. Sometimes, you may find that you put up barriers to try to stop yourself moving forward – by *creating* an illness. This is one of the more destructive elements contained within the 1 energy. But one which can eventually lead to positive results because as you release your resistance you may find that your life moves you forward even faster than before. For example, if you are ill because you were mentally stressed and you resisted exercising, then when you release your resistance you may exercise even more and perhaps enjoy it more too.

In terms of possible health complaints, adrenal stress is one of the more common challenges in a 1 Personal Year cycle. Your adrenals govern your 'flight or fight' mechanisms (how your react to stress, that is by ignoring it or by dealing with it head on). You may also have a tendency towards digestive problems this year, as a result of the challenges of 'digesting' the new situations that come your way, or breaking down old psychological patterns of behaviour or situations that you are facing.

The advantages of being influenced by a 1 as your Personal Year, Month, Week or Day cycle is that this 1 energy helps to break down patterns which are no longer serving you. For example, being ignorant is one pattern which may mean you are not as healthy as you potentially could be. By being ignorant or unaware of what constitutes a healthy mind, body and spirit, you are unable to work towards it. Breaking down patterns means you can rebuild them in a particular way, and by doing this it can help you to move forward with your life and help you to stay healthy too.

PERSONAL YEAR
2

To move into a 2 Personal Year you have been through the 1 to 9 Personal Year cycles, completed a year of new beginnings and have now arrived at the 2 which highlights balance. Under the influence of this 2 cycle you are working towards achieving balance with your health too. This may mean that you become more aware of balancing your diet (what you eat and drink) according to your body type, or aware of the amount of exercise you do (or not) during an average week. You may also become aware of needing to balance your emotions, and bring balance and harmony into your life generally.

The number 2 is particularly related to the emotions and if you already have this number in your chart then issues surrounding them can be intensified during this Personal Year. With the 2's influence, for example, you may become more aware of your emotional needs. Perhaps you feel supported by those close to you and therefore feel safe to open up even more to them emotionally. Or perhaps you realize that you need more emotional support from those around you. However, sometimes when you feel a lack of support emotionally it may be because others feel that they can't open up to you because you are not being open with them. This 2 energy can help you to loosen up any blocked emotions, for instance, when you have been fearful to open up emotionally to somebody for a long time it can help you. During this Personal Year you may find it easier to express your feelings to people gently without losing your cool.

The 2 energy can help to bring out your caring and nurturing instincts towards yourself and others. For example, if you have been so over-focused on your work in your previous Personal Year 1 you may suddenly develop an intense interest in looking after your health which includes your emotions. Perhaps you go to bed earlier or make sure you get a balanced amount of sleep (the right amount of hours for you) so that emotionally you feel better during the day. When you are tired, with the influence of the 2, you are more likely to be moody and this can rub off on those around you. So caring for yourself is helpful.

During this year perhaps you give too much to others emotionally and this can contribute to your health going out of balance as you forget to look after yourself emotionally. Sensitivity is one quality contained within the potential of this number, and you may find that you emotionally 'take on' others feelings too. For example, you may see a friend who is in crisis, and you can really feel their pain, so much so that because you want to help him or her you take *their* pain away with you. During this 2 year cycle it may help you to learn to be aware which feelings are yours and which feelings are others'.

Paradoxically, you may also give too much attention to your emotions and become preoccupied with every little feeling, which contributes towards an imbalance in your health. Health is about balancing your mind, body and spirit. However, by giving to others emotionally it can actually help you to stay healthy as you learn to focus attention on others' feelings for a while and not just your own. A 2 is asking you to give, which can really help you. The 2 is an energy which asks you to be aware of two people in any situation. When you are aware of others' feelings it may actually help you to stay calm and centred.

With a 2 influencing your health you may also find that emotional issues get out of hand and you become so sensitive and emotional that you find it challenging to function at full capacity. Perhaps you are too busy expressing all those (locked away) emotions, or you may be an emotional person anyway, which intensifies during this 2 Personal Year.

Life is a balancing act and when your health goes out of balance you may feel like you cannot cope with its ups and downs as well as when you feel calm and collected. When you are calm and balanced this reflects out into all areas of your life, including your health.

With a 2 influencing this Personal Year you may find that you become very fearful of becoming ill. Perhaps you remember when you were ill or even emotionally unbalanced in the past, and fear this happening again. Fear of illness can actually contribute towards it materializing because fears are resistances which when measured in energy push up against the very thing you fear. It may therefore help you to face your fears this year to help you avoid creating unnecessary illness.

Other fears in your life can also create an imbalance in your health; for example, fear of spiders, fear of rejection, and so on. However, the more love there is in your life the less place there is for fear, so opening up to your feelings of love from your environment, and loving yourself can also help you to stay balanced and healthy too.

Number 2 highlights the need for decision-making and during this Personal Year you can learn to make decisions which will help to keep you healthy and happy. For example, you may decide to leave an emotionally draining situation with a lover and find a loving and caring partner to share your life with instead. Bringing positive energy into your life can help you to stay healthy. You may also make a decision to turn down a career which would demand too much from you emotionally on a daily basis (particularly if you are very sensitive already), like caring for the sick or infirm for example. Everyone goes through times when their emotions are turned upside down and back again, but choosing to make decisions which can help you to stay emotionally balanced in the long run can really help your whole health.

Under the influence of the 2 in your Personal Year you may also find you get sick when you are faced with decision-making. You may try to use an illness as a way of avoiding choosing between one situation or another, or indeed as a way to get someone else to make a decision for you. Perhaps an illness allows you to open up emotionally to others, or enables you to get some loving attention from those around you. However, in a 2 cycle you may find that situations keep coming back to you over and over again in order to allow you to flex your decision-making muscles, so the sooner you learn the better your health may be.

Being emotional can be very wearing indeed and during this 2 year cycle you may find yourself tired, weary and drained as a result of all this emotional activity. If, however, you learn to balance your emotions you may find that during a 2 Personal Year you feel particularly placid and calm, with life moving along at a gentle pace. Perhaps your life during this period is a mixture of both.

Because your emotions are highlighted this year then health problems associated with your hormones may be more prevalent. For example, if you are a woman, you may have bigger mood swings around the time of menstruation or become more emotional generally with PMT. You may also have a tendency towards skin rashes or skin sensitivities like eczema. Perhaps you may find that you have illnesses associated with your breathing like asthma, chesty bronchitis from time to time, and so on. Yoga and breathing exercises may help you during this year to stay calm and balanced.

Learning to find emotional balance can really contribute towards your overall well-being and health during this 2 year cycle.

PERSONAL YEAR

3

If you are influenced by a 3 Personal Year cycle this means that you have come through the 1 cycle of new beginnings and of new starts, and the 2 cycle where you were working towards balancing your health. During this 3 cycle you are being asked to expand your life in some way and in terms of your health this may, for example, mean expanding upon your levels of physical fitness, and so on.

Expansion is a term which highlights a moving forward in a way which brings a moving out into life (rather than a contracting inwards). In terms of your health, if at times, during your last cycle you were able to balance your emotions and health, then during this cycle you may be able to expand on this and find it easier to do so for longer periods of time. The number 3 highlights self-expression, so if you have learned to open yourself up emotionally to others (in your last 2 cycle) in this 3 Personal Year you may be able to express these emotions more easily. Similarly, if in your 2 Personal Year you learned to swim ten lengths of the swimming pool every day, then this year you may be able to swim fifteen or twenty lengths, and so on. You can feel a great satisfaction from expansion because it helps you to grow in confidence, which can help to boost your body with positive energy too.

Conversely, you may find expansion a challenge to your health because it can mean that you try to do too much too quickly. For example, with a 3 you may be influenced to ride your bicycle for hours on end on your first jaunt out, because you are so laid back and are enjoying yourself thoroughly (other attributes of the 3). However, each number contains an element of the number before and after it. Therefore with a 2 influencing this 3 cycle, it can help you to find a balance at times when you are racing off into life at a hundred miles an hour.

The number 3 highlights the quality of easiness, and this year you may find it easier to say or do things which were previously great challenges to you. If you have been ill for a long time it may mean that you find it easier to handle the illness during this 3 cycle, or if you get ill this year you may make less fuss than before, or just let go of worrying. If you do become ill in a 3 year this may be because you are putting up resistance to expanding yourself. You may feel like there is nowhere for you to expand to, no avenues left untried, so with no focus you may get ill. However, all illness is there to teach you something about yourself, and even by getting sick you are expanding your life in some way because you are growing in self awareness, even if it doesn't seem like a good experience during this time.

With a 3 influencing this Personal Year confidence is highlighted. For example, you may feel able to put your body into an itsy-bitsy bikini and walk on the beach (even without in your own eyes having the perfect figure), and so on. With this 3 energy you can really learn to let go and do things without criticizing yourself all the time, which is another attribute of the number 3. Of course you may not always succeed, and then you may well criticize and reprimand yourself thoroughly. Negative criticism can contribute towards ill health and with the influence of the 3, you can learn to simply let things go, and let life flow. It may help you to say, 'So what, I only worked out in the gym for fifty minutes today!' and walk away knowing you did your best.

During a 3 Personal Year cycle you may be influenced to be too carefree about your health and you may find health problems build up and worsen more than you expect. For example, if you haven't visited your dentist for a check-up in years then you may find that this year your teeth or gums have deteriorated, and you may need more than just a simple filling when toothache triggers your next appointment. Of course failing to look after your teeth can contribute towards an overall lack of well-being too, and as with all illnesses, one simple thing out of balance affects the whole.

You may find, particularly if you are a serious person, that during a 3 cycle its energy can help you to lighten up, or you can learn to let go and laugh at yourself and at life more often. Laughter and fun can help you to stay healthy because laughing helps to release stress from your body. Laughter lightens and then permeates through into your whole life. It has been said that laughter can help to bring temporary pain relief to those with even serious health complaints. Whether you are ill or not, during a 3 Personal Year you may be uplifted by the joy of laughter which is certainly one of the best healers to include on a daily basis in your life this year.

During a 3 cycle you may become more sensitive to life and this may improve your health. For example, you may become more aware that you are overdoing things in your life (particularly if you have a 3 in your chart already) and this awareness may lead you to take appropriate action to improve your life and health. This 3 energy can soften you up so you become more sensitive to others' needs, and this can have a positive influence over your health as you feel more at ease with people.

With a 3 influencing your Personal Year you can find that you try to focus your energies on too many different things at once. For example, you may be eating breakfast, reading the daily newspaper, talking on the telephone all at once, which results in a lack of concentration on either activity. When you scatter your energies outward in all directions, it can mean that there is not enough energy left in the present to keep you focused and well. Have you ever noticed that you get sick just when there is so much (too much) to do or when there's a lot going on in your life? It is literally like there are little bits of yourself scattered around which you need to draw back in. Sometimes, meditation or learning to still your mind, even for short periods during each day, can really help to bring you back to the present and give you the energy to carry on. Focusing on a picture with lovely green trees in it or a deep blue lake, or even going out in the garden for a few moments, can all help to reconnect you with yourself and focus you in the present.

A 3 may influence you to become more tactile, and lots of hugs can help you to stay healthy too. Massage can also help to calm you down and to still your active mind, and keep you in one place for more than a few minutes if you do find yourself running around doing everything at once.

During a 3 cycle you may get mental exhaustion as a result of being confused about which activity to carry out next. For example, perhaps you go into conflict about whether to do your work or go out for a long walk. Mental exhaustion can also arise out of thinking too much about a situation instead of taking actions to resolve it. Sometimes when you get to the point of mental exhaustion you may find gentle exercise can help you think more clearly. Of course being in a 3 Personal Year means you may want your head to sort itself quicker than it logically can, and the 3 can then teach you to let go and let life and health sort themselves out in their own time. If you try to force things in a

3 Personal Year you may end up fraught with even more frustration and stress which can affect your overall health.

During a 3 Personal Year you may develop a tendency towards circulatory problems, muscular aches, and mental stress, so looking after yourself in these areas can help.

PERSONAL YEAR
4

During a 4 Personal Year you have worked through three cycles of this 9 year cycle already. You have worked through the new opportunities of the 1 cycle, have been learning to balance your life in the 2 cycle and to bring expansion into your life during the 3 cycle. This 4 cycle is a time for consolidating all that you have learned in these past 3 cycles. For example, in terms of your health, if you took up a new exercise routine, saw it as a challenge in the 1 cycle, balanced it with your routine in the 2 cycle, developed a more advanced workout in the 3 cycle, then this year you have the opportunity to consolidate all of these. Perhaps this year, after working for three years to get physically fit, your body may become much stronger.

The number 4 influences structure and in this 4 cycle you may find that an illness can shake your very foundations and you struggle with your health and life at times. This is because the number 4 highlights the physical level, and making physical changes can be very challenging. However, sometimes old structures need to be brought down and reorganized to make you stronger in the long run – the way a builder pulls down some walls in a building to rearrange them to make the building safer and more solid. One of the ways you can help to strengthen your structure is by body-building, working out in the gym, or even simply by walking, and so on.

As the 4 particularly influences your physical body you may notice that your body shape or weight changes this year; perhaps your body takes on a more solid appearance. With the influence of the 4, paradoxically your body may even become weaker in appearance as you resist life and refuse to pay attention to its physical needs. For example, as a result of eating irregular meals, or because your only exercise is walking from the car to the front door, and so on. During this year you may find challenges in other areas influence your health as you are too busy sorting them out to pay attention to your physical needs.

During this 4 Personal Year it is essential for you to pay great attention to your physical body's needs in order to help you to stay healthy. Therefore a good diet, exercise, fresh air, love and sex can all contribute to your overall well-being. However, the mind and emotions also influence your physical health so being aware of feeding these can help.

With the influence of the 4 you may become more practical this year and are able to deal with opportunities and challenges to your health in a step-by-step manner. If you decide to structure your work, social, and family life in order to fit your new exercise routine in, then it may mean you simply implement these changes a little at a time. With a 4, bringing in changes slowly can sometimes mean the difference between you persevering with something, or giving up because the changes are simply too much for you to handle. There is a saying 'You need to learn to walk before you can run' and this particularly applies to your health and your life during this 4 Personal Year. Simply take things a step at a time.

Responsibility is a key word associated with the human race, which in numerology is influenced by the number 4. Therefore this year is a key time for you to learn to take responsibility for yourself. So if you overdo things and your health bears the consequences then learn by your experiences and take responsibility for your actions. For example, if you overdo your jogging session then your aching feet will eventually heal and soothe, but if you overdo all areas of your life it can have a strong bearing on your physical health. Sometimes, by taking responsibility for your life your health can improve. However, every experience you have can teach you about responsibility and it is up to you to learn the lessons if you choose.

With the influence of the 4 you may be irresponsible at times, and you may therefore get sick because you were just not paying enough attention to life. For example, perhaps you forgot to read the instructions when cooking some food and it gives you stomach ache. This is an additional incident which gives you the message that you are not fully grounded in the present.

With a Personal Year influence of 4 you may also create an illness at times this year to help you ground yourself and bring you back down to earth (qualities of the 4). For example, if you have been over-exercising and straining your body and you injure your foot so that you are forced to rest, then this can influence you to be more practical about what exercises you perform next time. It can help you to be more realistic about what you can and can't do in relation to your health.

In a 4 Personal Year you may suddenly develop a passion for looking after your body, paying attention to grooming, taking more interest in what you wear, your haircut, make-up and so on. Perhaps you visit the chiropodist to perk up your feet, have a manicure; you may feel you want to look neat. When you look good you often feel good too, and when you feel safe and secure from within you often feel good about your outer physical appearance too. Feeling positive about who you are and how you look even for a short time can have a positive influence on your overall health and well-being.

Sometimes in a 4 Year you may suddenly feel the urge to take more risks. For example, if you have previously been generally lazy in your attitude towards your diet or exercise then you may take a big risk and decide to design yourself a new health regime. Because the 4 influences the use of routine and order to help bring a sense of security into your life, then implementing even small changes to your routine may seem a big risk indeed. However, you can choose to make a drama (4 quality) out of these changes or you may decide to simply give it your best shot by approaching the risk positively and with a down-to-earth attitude. Either way, some risks pay off and some risks don't but in the long run at least you put in the effort. The 4 energy influences determination and you may give yourself a long time before you give up on a new diet, exercise or lifestyle which can help to improve your health.

With a 4 you may get sick when you feel there are too many dramas going on in your life, at work, for example, or in your home life. This may be a way of you opting out of taking responsibility and sorting out these situations. Perhaps you also create an illness to give someone else the chance to learn more about responsibility too. For instance, if you are always in charge at work then being off sick for a time means that your deputy can learn more about responsibility as well. However, a key reason for your illness may be because you have taken on far too many responsibilities and you cannot handle the heavy load. Being ill then gives you the chance to decide whether you are too good at being responsible for others and whether you need to allow them to take care of their own responsibilities, and what to do about this.

You may have a tendency towards kidney or bladder problems during this cycle, and you may also feel heavy, down or depressed as a result of working through key physical issues in your life. Working through these issues by taking responsibility for yourself can also help you to balance the spiritual, mental, emotional and physical levels of your body.

PERSONAL YEAR
5

In a 5 Personal Year you have come through new beginnings (1), balance (2), expansion (3) and grounding (4) and now the 5 energy is helping to bring movement and change into your life. In your last cycle of a 4 Personal Year you can get too bogged down or preoccupied with your physical health and so this 5 cycle can help to move you on.

The number 5 is a fast-moving energy which can influence changes in your health and life literally to happen overnight. For example, you suddenly see the light that you need to quit smoking or cut down on alcohol or chocolate intake, and you may decide on the spot to do something about it. This can arise from a sudden impulse to improve or change your life as a result of listening to your intuition, which may be stronger and clearer during this 5 cycle. The 5 also brings in qualities from deep within your soul which may be guiding you with your life. At other times the inspiration to improve your health may come from the logical brain which may be telling you, 'If I carry on eating too many cream cakes at once then I'll get sick.'

You may be influenced by the factual elements contained within the number 5. You may like to find out, for example, exactly how changing your diet can affect you. Perhaps you read every ingredient on the food packaging before you buy it, or before taking a gym class speak to people who have done it to see how it has benefited them. The 5 means that if you are sometimes 'airy-fairy' then it can help you to see the logic behind your thoughts and actions and help to bring you down to earth.

The 5 can also influence you to feel sceptical towards your health. This may mean you do not believe you can become healthier, or that you have the power to improve your health. However, scepticism can be helpful in some ways because when you do prove to yourself that you can, for example, cut down on coffee, then the facts speak for themselves and may help you to believe in your body's healing abilities. It is only when scepticism prevents you from even trying that this can sometimes become a destructive factor in your life.

Of course in a 5 Personal Year you may also procrastinate (a 5 quality) about making any changes to your physical health for a while. Perhaps you say 'just another cigarette' or 'just another biscuit – I'll give up tomorrow' except that tomorrow never comes and may just be like today. Another chance to sit and think about the changes you wish to make in your life. However, once you have made up your mind (another aspect of the 5 energy) to do something you may move forward at the speed of light.

If you have a 5 in your chart already you can be very changeable about which methods to use to help improve your health. You may decide to study art history to stimulate your mind. If you are passionate about this subject this may produce a positive effect on your health. Typical of the 5 energy, you may become restless halfway through the course and switch to another tutorial. Perhaps you also switch from playing tennis to cycling, or swimming to rafting, and so on. However, the 5 energy is also asking you to learn to be adaptable and most exercises or training of the mind can help you to bring some positive focus into your life which can therefore help to boost your energy within it. So on days when you may find yourself so changeable that you procrastinate and don't get things done, it can help to bring out its elements of structure and organisation to help you get through.

In a 5 Personal Year it can bring out your abilities to instruct others, and you may find yourself demonstrating to your friends how to do aerobics, pilates, or how to do certain exercises. Indeed, the 5 brings in the quality of clarity and you may find that your abilities to communicate clearly to others this year is heightened too, which may be why people choose to flock to you for assistance. The influence of the 5 may also mean that you keep asking your gym instructor over and over again how, why, what and where he or she is doing, until you get clarity about what you are trying to perform. As the 5 influences movement then you may decide to take up dancing this year, and perhaps you like to know exactly how to work out each movement in a sequence or how to do a specific dance. Flamenco dancing may also appeal during this 5 Year cycle because it is very fast and energetic, adventurous and exciting, which can help stimulate your mind, body and spirit.

During a 5 year you may even take adventure to its limits and, for example, instead of swimming your normal amount of lengths in the pool each day you want to swim the English Channel and be really daring. This may challenge you mentally and physically and you may enjoy this because it adds a spark of fun to your life, but with the 5 life can throw up the unexpected at times. Perhaps your zest for life this year means that your health takes a downward spin for a time. Indeed you can get sick from being over-adventurous during a 5 cycle, but your health can also decline from a lack of energy and stimulation if you don't have some adventures in your life too. Of course adventure can be simply eating some different foods for dinner which may also stimulate and boost your energies without having to swim the Channel.

In a 5 Personal Year you may find that there are many changes to your life and particularly if these changes are big and sudden, you may become ill. Sometimes you get ill during times of great change so that you can take time off to internalize and work out the changes a little in your mind. When you are ill you are often more open to listen to your intuition too, and to follow through on some of the things which may help you with your life and your health. Change is a certainty in life and life changes from moment to moment and you may be even more aware of the quality of change within your lifestyle and health during a 5 Personal Year.

During a 5 cycle you may try to restrict your workout routines or your diet in some way, in order to help you stay in control of lots of external changes within your environment. For example, if you have too much pressure, change and commitments at work then you may restrict the amount of time you spend at the gym, or fail to prepare yourself a good meal when you get home at the end of the day. Over a period of time these restrictions may influence your overall well-being and you may even find that you are too tired or unable to do the same amount of things in a day as you regularly do. You may become ill if you restrict looking after your body even for a short time. Restrictions can help you so that things don't get too out of hand (too much exercise is not necessarily beneficial for you either). By placing some restrictions here and there it may actually mean that your home life, social life, love and sex life, family life and health and fitness life can find a balance.

The 5 energy means that you may have a tendency towards accidents this year – as you quickly change your mind from one moment to the next about which direction you are heading off in. You may also develop throat problems because the 5 is associated with communication and one way to avoid that is to lose your voice!

The number 5 highlights change, and choosing to view change in a positive way can really help your well-being.

PERSONAL YEAR
6

You are now influenced by a 6 Personal Year cycle which means that you are in the final year of working out your main physical experiences which will form the basis of this current 9 Year cycle. So in this year you have been through the 1 to 5 cycles and learned about some of the potential qualities contained within those numbers and you are now ready to move on.

The number 6 highlights wholeness and therefore during a 6 Personal Year you may be even more aware of what this constitutes in terms of your health. For example, wholeness may mean you work out the best possible food or diet for yourself which also helps your family's health too. This is because during this cycle you may have more of an awareness about the group needs and not just your own. Perhaps your family or friends always go for a long walk on a Sunday after lunch and therefore you may join in with them. Your health interests may in some ways be tied in with a group of people you are close to, and with the influence of the 6 you may enjoy being and doing things in groups. This may also mean that if you decide to start a new diet or work in some extra exercises to your regular workout then your family, friends or group members may also be involved or be encouraged to do the same. This may well serve and help the whole group to stay healthy and fit too.

With wholeness as a presiding quality during this period you may also decide to find wholeness within the foods you eat. Perhaps you choose to buy more fresh fruit and vegetables to eat, or buy the best organic foods you can find. You may even decide to take a cookery course during this cycle to help you understand more ways in which you can find wholeness from the foods you eat. Perhaps you decide to give up eating masses of junk food in this 6 cycle, or indeed if your diet is already full of good foods or wholefoods then a bit of junk food may possibly help to balance out your diet in some way.

The 6 energy highlights obsessions and in a 6 Personal Year, particularly if this number is in your chart already, you may get carried away and obsessed with food, exercise and even your health. Sometimes your obsession with doing a certain exercise or sport over and over again means that you may develop repetitive strain injury. Obsessions mean that you go very deeply into something one hundred per cent, and doing this may eventually help you to find wholeness or feel complete within yourself. For example, if you decide to take up tennis during this cycle you may find that in the extreme you play every spare hour of your waking life and when you stop you read about tennis or watch play on television, and so on. One day you may just wake up and think 'I've had enough' and decide you've had your fill for one lifetime. This learning experience then becomes integrated into your whole being and it is something with which you may indeed feel totally complete.

When you focus all your attention on your health or on an ailment it may sometimes get worse because you are giving it too much of your energy which then contributes towards it manifesting itself. Finding a balance by focusing on all the areas in your life can help you to stay healthy as this brings in the quality of wholeness.

During a 6 Personal Year you may like to eat foods that comfort you and make you feel good, because the 6 highlights the emotional level of your body, which you may feel the need to satisfy through your diet. You may feel like you simply can't eat enough to fulfil your emotional neediness and at other times you may feel overstuffed with foods from trying to smother down some emotions within you. Again, bringing in the quality of wholeness and finding other aspects contained within the whole picture can help to fulfil your emotional needs. For example, talking over your feelings with your partner, friends or someone close to you may help, or writing down your feelings in a diary can help to release some emotions, and so on.

As a result of your sensitivity you may also neglect to eat and nurture yourself during this 6 year cycle. Perhaps you neglect your own emotional needs because you are too busy satisfying everyone else's, which can influence your health. When you neglect your health your whole life can be affected, but this experience may also show you what it is you need to do in order to restore a sense of well-being and wholeness in your life.

If you do find yourself under the weather during this 6 year cycle it does provide you with the opportunity to go deeply inside of yourself to explore the deeper meaning to the illness and to why situations are occurring in your life. Sometimes you may really appreciate the time and space an illness gives you to be able to contact this magical inner space. You may not always want to get sick of course, but by being positive about what it can teach you it can help you to really grow.

The 6 highlights issues connected with your emotions and your heart and therefore an illness may also be one way you can learn to open your heart to yourself, particularly if you regularly avoid dealing with your feelings. This cycle can therefore help you to get closer to others too, and to open your heart to them. Love makes the world go around, and it melts away the pain and fear of past experiences which may be blocking you finding health and happiness. The more love that you can bring into your life and the lives of those around you the more joy you can feel from within. This can have a positive influence over your health and your whole life.

Within this 6 year cycle you may be working strongly with the quality of commitment – you may learn what it's like to be committed to keeping yourself healthy and fit. For example, the 6 may influence you to start looking after yourself and to be good to yourself, and it may feel great for a day, but getting up on a rainy morning to go for a jog around the block may not be your idea of fun. Yes, you can be flexible and allow yourself a morning off but it is your long-term commitment which can help to keep you healthy. When you commit to looking after yourself you may find others want to love and look after you too because they can see you respect and love yourself. This then brings more love and more caring into the world which can help you to become even healthier.

In a 6 year cycle you may find yourself getting sick because you are trying to avoid making commitments, or avoid carrying through the commitments that you have already made. For example, you may get sick before an important exam, or before your driving test, or get sick to avoid meeting a new date, or to avoid an important life-changing work interview. By facing your commitments and only making commitments you intend to keep, it can help your whole being as these positive energies freely circulate through your mind, body and spirit.

With the influence of this 6 energy in your life during this Personal Year you may have a tendency towards hormonal problems such as PMT, if you are a woman, or emotional stress. Perhaps you find it easier to express your emotions this year, or find that you express them more whether you like it or not. This 6 energy may help you to get in contact with buried emotions and old hurts and pains which can help to free up blockages in your whole energy system. Therefore you may actually feel a sense of emotional well-being and happiness during this cycle. Sometimes, painting or playing a musical instrument (or listening to music) are lovely ways for you to contact and express your emotions too.

PERSONAL YEAR
7

Within the cycles 1 to 9 the 7th cycle is the completion and the culmination of the events and experiences that you have learned about during your previous 6 years. In numerology this means that if you have worked to maintain your health, whether that be physical, emotional, mental or spiritual health, then during this cycle it is possible for you to reap the rewards from your positive endeavours. For example, if you have been exercising regularly during the past 6 cycles, then in this 7 year your body may physically be toned up, which can help to bring a stabilizing influence over your health and life.

If, however, you have neglected your health overall during the last 6 years then you may notice that you become more sensitive to illness during this 7 Personal Year. Your body may even break down (infections, emotional breakdown, general weakness, and so on) because you have neglected it. The number 7 is particularly associated with health issues, and so it is asking you this year to pay attention to your health, and issues which are contributing towards your lifestyle.

You may suddenly decide in a 7 Personal Year to take great care of your mind, body and spirit. The 7 energy contains a little of the 6 energy (and 8) within it. This number 6 highlights nurturing and caring and these qualities can be brought out to encourage you to apply them to your life.

Sometimes during this 7 cycle you may feel very vulnerable and feel too open to life, and perhaps you take on others' emotions. The number 7 energy highlights great emotional sensitivity, which is a gift too, and by being aware of using your mind to steady your emotions when you are feeling all wobbly then it may help you to keep a grip on life. Of course, if you are a person who has neglected (another quality of the 6's influence over the 7) your feelings, particularly for a long time, then your emotions may simply crack open during this 7 Personal Year cycle.

Sometimes you may get taken in by your own emotions and feel things which aren't real. For example, you have a pain in your left knee and you feel it's something really serious when in fact it is a simple bruise which is causing the distress (although of course you get it checked out by your GP). When your emotions are out of balance with the rest of your life then this can influence your overall health to go out of balance too. In a 7 Personal Year it may be help-ful to be gentle with yourself and to allow your feelings to arise as a natural part of your daily process. And at the same time getting on with your life, so that your emotions don't control (an 8 quality, a little of which is influencing this 7 cycle) your life.

One of the issues highlighted during this cycle is that of pain. However, pain can be very useful. Physical pain can tell you when some part of your body is sick and needing attention, so that you can do something practical about it if you choose. Emotional pain also gives you clues to circum-stances which are contributing towards creating that pain, perhaps offering psychological patterns of behaviour for you to observe and work with. With the influence of the 7 you may also feel mental pain and anxieties as a result of not trusting the process of life. Finally you may also feel spiri-tual pain, particularly if you feel isolated (a 7 quality) or disconnected from others during this cycle.

Pain has many uses and is a valuable tool, but when you resist pain it usually exacerbates it until sometimes the pain becomes almost unbearable. Pain is reminding you of the parts of yourself which are not yet integrated into your life, and are therefore separated off from deep within yourself. For example, if you feel emotional pain about your mother who walked out on you when you were a small child then that pain may feel like a 'thing' inside you. You do not like that pain (naturally) and so you treat it like an impostor – 'it' versus 'me'. Any type of pain is a calling to go inside yourself and to reconnect with even the darkest shadows within. This can help the pain to melt away as you become at one with it, or indeed with yet another part of yourself.

In a 7 Personal Year you may feel all the pain from the previous 6 year cycles, or indeed from all the 9 year cycles before that, which are returning to you on some level. Of course working on personal issues is like peeling an onion; with each layer you go deeper and deeper. So you heal the superficial levels first until eventually you may touch on the very core of your issue. During each 7 year cycle you have the opportunity to delve in as deep as you choose to go; it is a healing process.

During this 7 Personal Year you may find that you have more energy and vitality and are generally more productive with your life as a result of releasing pent-up emotions and pain. This can influence your health positively, as letting go of blockages in your body helps to balance your mind, body and spirit. You may discover that you get things done faster, like your morning exercises just seem to flow, or your body feels lighter and you may physically get around much faster, and so on.

The number 7 energy contains a strong spiritual element within it. If you have been focusing your attention (particularly in the previous 6 year cycle) on the purely physical health aspects (like exercise, food, and so on), then your health may go out of sync during this cycle. Spirituality is about your connection to your inner or higher self, and your connection to others (to the whole of humanity). It is the inner spiritual light of love which makes your eyes sparkle even when you are not physically at your peak. Sometimes physical exercise can help to connect you to yourself (the sort where it seems like a meditative process), but meditation and t'ai chi and breathing exercises can help you to reconnect as well. If you are going through great stress in your life then going deep within yourself to do some soul-searching may contribute towards keeping your health in balance.

You may find your health is delicate at times. Perhaps you catch colds easier or feel tired more often, and so on . . . You may even feel feeble as you try to resist illness and pain. Working with any illness by focusing on the positive things in life may help you to stay calm and centred even when you are ill.

You may become unwell to avoid facing the actuality of living in the real world. Perhaps you cannot face challenges with your job, or within a relationship, for example. However, when you are ill this creates a space for you to be able to introspect and to reconnect so that you can find ways of facing reality again. With the 7 energy you may also find that you become ill as a result of too much introspection and from losing your grip on reality by escaping into your imagination. For example by dwelling on some problem within your mind and avoiding dealing with it in the physical world. Too much time spent inside yourself means you can get 'lost' and feel depressed when it is time for you to come out into the real world. A little physical exercise or a gentle walk may help to ground you back into everyday life, and helps to keep you healthy too.

You may have a tendency towards panic attacks, perhaps as a result of your fear of living in the real world. Therefore, particularly at times when you are feeling anxious, you may also be prone to breathing difficulties. Perhaps you may be a little neurotic at times about your health as you can become preoccupied with every physical ache and pain.

There may be a big opportunity to bring together all the wonderful lessons you have learned in the past and to help produce a wonderful and healthy mind, body and spirit.

PERSONAL YEAR
8

You have come through the 6 cycles of physical experience, the 7th cycle of production or loss, and you are now influenced by the 8 in your Personal Year cycle. The 8 highlights the need for re-evaluation, particularly of your last 7 year cycles, to see how, what, and whether you would like to change things in your current cycle. For example, if you have been very active in maintaining your physical fitness and health during the last 7 years then during this cycle you may decide to change your regime for a new one. Perhaps you see that some minor adjustments are now needed in your life to help keep you fit as a result of external situations which are changing too.

Re-evaluating your health status is helpful because it means that you are not allowing your life to get stale. For example, you may jog four miles every day when you are seventeen or even twenty-six, but when you are thirty-five or forty-four you may not find this easy. Therefore, if there was no re-evaluating of capabilities and performance then you may carry on with the same old routine which may run you down or even contribute towards making you ill eventually. Re-evaluation is therefore a time to take stock of where you are in life, and it is an essential tool which can help you with your growth and personal development. Re-evaluating allows you to see what needs to be let go of within this 8 Personal Year cycle in order to help keep you healthy and help you to balance your life.

Cutting the ties with the past can help to keep you healthy because it frees up energy or parts of yourself which are still attached to those situations. If you went through a major illness sometime during the previous 7 years and you are still, for instance, angry about it, then this can contribute towards your ill health right now. Living in the past blocks energy available to you now, so during this 8 year you may choose to revaluate your thoughts around past situations in order to help improve your general well-being.

With an 8 influencing you this year you may suddenly decide to start taking your health seriously. Perhaps you have been fortunate to have generally good health and you have realized that it is time to contribute towards your maintenance. Perhaps you decide to lose a few pounds, tone up, sharpen up your brain power and so on. The 8 influences the will to do things, and this can help you to follow through on your decisions. It is also a number which asks you to work to strengthen your will, and, paradoxically, you may be weak-willed and give up more easily when it comes to your overall health this year too. Sometimes when you see results it gives you the will to go on. So if you have decided to cut down from five cups of coffee a day to two and you already notice the difference to your health, then your will can drive you on. Of course you may also develop the capacity and the will to drink even more coffee too, to please your own ego about just what you term as 'good' for you. With an 8 you may become stubborn and will not be told what is or isn't good for you!

With an 8 influencing this Personal Year you may find that you take yourself terribly seriously, particularly if you have this number in your chart already. Your ego may be bruised in your jog down the street in your designer sportswear, only to find that people laugh at the sight of your knobbly knees or lack of physical fitness as you crawl through the park. Therefore the 8 can help to teach you to be aware of your inner health, which is equally if not more important than how you dress or what you look like.

An 8 Personal Year influences you to build up your inner and outer strength. Inner strength comes from the spiritual will which moves through you and in some ways governs your life, and your outer strength comes from your inner strength too. Of course it is also necessary to build a strong physical body as a means to externalize this inner strength, and in an 8 year this is just what you may be aiming to do. With an 8 it may mean that you are influenced to look after your mind, body and spirit in an all-or-nothing way. For example, you may one day meditate, exercise, eat well, and the next day do none of these at all, as you range from active to totally passive. It may help you to incorporate some of the 7 energy (a little is contained within the 8) into your life to bring in gentleness, so that you can learn to do things in a gentle, and not in an intense way.

You may become unwell when you are revisiting past situations because they may bring back memories which you would rather leave buried. Perhaps the illness helps you to release all the stress associated with these situations too. In an 8 year you have the opportunity to find the strength to deal with the past so that you can become healthier and happier.

Illnesses, particularly if you have an 8 in your chart already, may be brought on as a result of karma from the past, or from your past lives. If you have, for example, refused to eat enough food to keep you healthy for many, many years then during an 8 year your karma may mean that you become weak or ill. Karma means you get back what you give out, and this applies to your thoughts and your intentions as well as to your actions. Similarly, if you have spent many lifetimes where you have worked hard to create a healthy physical body or mind, then this karma may well be paid back during this lifetime. You may be very bright and successful with your mind, or a great athlete, for example. You create your karma on a daily basis and never more can you be potentially aware of this than during your current 8 year cycle.

You may also be unwell at times this year as a way of avoiding taking on responsibilities, particularly karmic ones. For example, you may have agreed to organize a charity run to raise money for a hospital threatened with closure as a result of financial strain. But at the last minute you create an illness which prevents you from carrying this responsibility through. Hence the charity concerned did not receive their final donation from you which they needed to save their hospital and it closes. (Perhaps this was their karma!) However, fate and your karma are always repaid; later on you may not have the money you need to buy essential medical supplies, for example. During this cycle lessons of karmic responsibilities may be hard and fast, but can eventually help you to let go and grow spiritually stronger.

Sometimes during this 8 cycle you may try to hold on to things and you may therefore be prone to constipation, or to diarrhoea if you are really letting go. The 8 is particularly associated with the mind and your thoughts influence your overall health. Thinking positive thoughts can therefore contribute towards your overall well-being during this 8 Personal Year cycle. In numerology 8 is also associated with the spine and joints, so you may find that health issues connected to these parts of your body may at times influence you during this cycle too.

The number 8 highlights the need to be responsible and everyone is constantly learning this lesson, but it is particularly heightened this year. Perhaps you suddenly become irresponsible about your health because you have been so over-burdened during the previous 7 year cycles that you just want a change. However, karma always steps in and no matter whether you think you deserve a better life or not, you get back exactly what you have put out, or put into creating a healthy mind, body and spirit.

PERSONAL YEAR
9

Every day you are learning the lessons you need in order for you to maintain a healthy life. Whether you are learning how to balance your mind, emotions, body or spirit, it all contributes towards your overall well-being. By the time you reach this 9 cycle, you have been working through new opportunities (1), balance (2), expansion (3), consolidation (4), movement (5), wholeness (6), materialization (7), re-evaluation (8) and you are now preparing yourself for your next completely new 9 year cycle.

This year you may feel like complete overhaul of your health. You may decide to go for a full medical, hire the services of a personal fitness trainer, visit a dietitian, change your physical appearance (your clothes, hair and so on), or go to a health retreat for a week.

James is an analyst for a financial institution and in his last Personal Year cycle 8 he got divorced, moved house, and also changed his career. In this 9 cycle he has joined a new gym which is near to his office and every day, without fail, he works out. James has noticed that doing exercise has really helped to inject positive energy into his whole life.

The number 9 highlights education and you may seek out people who can inspire you with their knowledge of ways in which you can look after yourself. For example, you may seek out a spiritual guru (teacher) who you can look to for spiritual guidance, or you may develop a keen interest in religion and go to church, or to a temple, or even spend time on an ashram, and so on. These things can help give you faith to go on, particularly if you feel a lack of direction within your life. You may also find great strength (an 8 quality, a little of which is contained within this 9 cycle) through following your own inner spiritual guidance this year too. You may decide to take up praying or using a mantra (a verse) to bring some positive energy into your life. Prayer is very powerful because each word carries with it thought forms which produce energy, therefore it is always helpful to choose your prayers carefully. Prayer can help to deepen your connection with your higher self. During this 9 cycle developing your spiritual connection with yourself and with others can help you to stay healthy.

Whatever you do during the 9 Personal Year you may really want to do it well because the 9 influences perfectionism; you can find yourself issuing incredibly high orders to yourself at times. For example, if you perform an exercise that does not live up to your standards or expectations you may get angry with yourself for the rest of the day. However, your mind may be willing but your body may not and you may demand more from yourself than your body can give. Your resolve may just give up on you at times, as you reach for a cake instead of the healthy food that you meticulously prepared for lunch. Being tough with yourself during this 9 cycle can at times support you to move forward and do things which can benefit your health, but being too tough means that you may just end up back at the beginning, and that's at number 1.

When you enter this 9 cycle it may seem like nothing is really happening and that outwardly there don't appear to be any great changes in your lifestyle, or to your health at all. This can be because you worked so hard on maintaining your health during your previous 8 year cycles that your health runs smoothly during this year. Perhaps much of the transformation needing to take place during this 9 cycle may be already in place so that your life simply flows along. Of course you still need to work at it, and keeping up the good work from the lessons you have learned from your last 8 years can benefit enormously.

However, you may just be tempted to let your hair down and let your health go during a 9 cycle, and refuse to put in any effort as you think you have done enough. As a result, you may become ill from not giving yourself enough care and attention. Indeed, you may not even care that much whether you are ill or not, as sometimes you just can't be bothered. You may develop this attitude as a result of dealing with some issues which are taking up a lot of your thinking space.

Influenced by the 9 in your Personal Year cycle, you may consciously or subconsciously feel a sense of relief that yet another 9 year cycle is complete and that you are moving on with your life. You may feel a loss of direction for a while or feel a great deal of emotion about moving on. In terms of your health, if you have not learned how to look after yourself fully during this last 9 years, then you know that there is, potentially, a whole new 9 year cycle to work through this again. This can be very exciting, and during this 9 year you may find or regain a sense of passion for exercise or healthy living (again).

With the influence of the 9 energy you may be more open to changing your lifestyle in some way in order to become healthier. For example, if you like to live in a conventional way, say by eating exactly what the social consensus believes is right for you, then this year you may say 'Blow it, I know what's best for me' and liberate yourself by eating exactly what you want. This 9 energy encourages you to be more open and flexible towards your health and lifestyle. Sometimes you can become too rigid (an 8 quality influencing this number 9) with your outlook on life, and over a period of time this can stagnate your energy and slow you down. Therefore with the 9 highlighting adaptability, this year can help you to let go, and let new things into your life, which can contribute towards your overall health and well-being.

During a 9 Personal Year you may find that you become unwell as a result of your selfless giving, because this 9 energy can encourage you to give and give to those around you. You may enjoy giving, and find you receive a lot of happiness from giving too, but sometimes you need to give to yourself, and an illness is one way of creating time alone. Indeed, you may also become ill if you find there is no one to give to or help out, but if you find yourself in this situation for a while it may be because you have earned a well-deserved rest to renew your energies! Therefore giving can also help to keep you healthy when you learn to give to yourself too.

During a 9 cycle you may also become ill because you are being too critical and judgmental of yourself, because of the constant lack of achievement in your life (you may actually achieve a lot but it is never good enough). By applying some of the easy-going and relaxed energy contained within this number 9 you can learn to accept that life can't always be perfect. Knowing this can help to release some of the pressure you place upon yourself. Of course an illness may develop when you find people are projecting too high expectations of you. For example, perhaps you are taking exams and your teacher has projected or forecast all 'A's for you, or your partner is expecting you to act in a certain way because his or her relatives are around. Life is always teaching you to be yourself, and the only way to learn about life is to be free to make your own mistakes and learn by experience through trial and error. Being yourself can help you to stay healthy and happy because you have no alter ego to live up to.

At times during this 9 year cycle you may have a tendency towards headaches, sinus pains, and you may also experience muscular aches and pains too. Perhaps your aches are from seeing or experiencing life in a new and different way now that you have come through to the end of this 9 year cycle.

2

PERSONAL YEARS AND YOUR CAREER

Within the Personal Year cycles 1 to 9 are highlighted potential trends which can influence you in your work or field, and can also influence you to take up a specific focus on your career path. For example, if you are entering a 3 Personal Year, particularly if you have the number 3 present in your chart already, you may find that you focus much attention on writing (one of its qualities). Perhaps you decide to write some music, or write more letters to people, or even take up a career in journalism. This means that during this 3 cycle your potential for developing that specific career or quality is strong. Therefore if it is something you would like to do, or have always wanted to do, if you put lots of practical effort and positive thinking towards your goals they are potentially more likely to be successful. Of course that is not to say that you suddenly write a blockbuster film overnight (although you may), but that you can progress on the path of your career or work choice.

There are many different terms to describe work. Your work may be your career, or just a job you perform each week. You may be a housewife and/or a mother, and this is work too. Perhaps you also describe your relationships as work, because you work on your relationships to help them work out. You probably work on your health to help keep you happy and healthy too.

Work and career are simply words to describe areas of focus in your life, and how you choose to live your life is your choice, along with the work you choose to focus on. In life, therefore, you can see that there are many areas of work, but in this chapter you can see areas within your work which are governing the 9 year cycles which influence you.

Also be aware that the larger cycles, that is the Universal Year cycles, play an important role in governing the kind of work you may choose during any specific year.

PERSONAL YEAR
1

The 1 is the beginning of a completely new 9 year cycle, therefore during this year it is a wonderful time to make new starts on work projects, to pursue a new career, or to find new or different aspects within your current work which you can enjoy. The 1 energy brings in fresh air to work situations so even if you are not consciously seeking to change your job then you may notice that things begin to change naturally. These changes can be challenging at times because even if you like moving on and trying new things, if something is different you may resist moving into that situation for a while.

During a 1 Personal Year life moves you forward, but you are also being asked to set your goals and to work positively towards them. For example, perhaps you would like to be promoted at work and this year by making clear the intention in your mind that this is what you would like, it can contribute towards making it happen. You may work harder to show that you are capable of the extra responsibilities that are associated with the new role. Perhaps one of the qualities needed for the promotion is that of leadership and therefore you demonstrate to your seniors that you are highly capable of this. The 1 energy highlights leadership and during this Personal Year it can help to bring out this quality from inside you, particularly if you show the potential already.

You may feel during this 1 cycle that you are being led, but with all the intent and purpose that can now drive you towards your goals it may well be your subconscious mind that is directing you. Perhaps deep inside you have always wanted to be the director of an orchestra, and although you are very musical you have not had any training in this field. However, perhaps you find yourself as an artist, designing the orchestra's leaflets which you have been asked to deliver to the administrator. Your next project as an artist may be to work on leaflets for one of the musicians within the orchestra. Eventually you may find life leading along a little path to the right door which opens up the opportunity for you to take on the job of your dreams. You may think this is coincidence, but it is called synchronicity, which means that all things are connected, and everything falls into place if and when they are meant to be.

In a 1 Personal Year you may find that you have a strong surge to move forward with your career or your work, and you may want things to literally change overnight. With the influence of the 1, when your goals take longer to materialize than you expect, you may get frustrated, and you may project more negative energy on to the very goals you want. Sometimes this can mean that your goals take longer to achieve as frustration and anger can contribute towards driving them away. However, the 1 Personal Year means that you are being asked to work towards your career goals, and some may materialize and others may even take a lifetime of hard work to achieve.

In the 1 Personal Year you can find that you lack focus (a quality of the 1) and this may be because you may constantly question your current work goals and direction, and so lose the focus on what you are currently occupied with. If you are a politician, for example, and you normally have strong specific views about a subject, then during this 1 year it may mean that you look at the same subject in a new light as you discover new information from your experiences. This may mean that as a politician you introduce these views to your constituency, or that you drop the subject altogether from your portfolio, or even that you give up your career in politics and focus on some other work instead.

With a 1 cycle you may lose your work focus for much of the year, and the larger the career move or the bigger the changes within your current job, the longer it may take you to adjust to moving forward with your life.

Sometimes, during a 1 Personal Year, new work opportunities may land on your doorstep; at other times you may have to seek them out. That is not to say that you take up these opportunities, of course, as starting new things may be a challenge to you. Perhaps you even lose good opportunities because you are indecisive (a quality of the 2 which influences the number 1). However, having a clear intention about what work you would really like to do can help you to take on the best possible opportunities.

With the 1 influencing your career you may feel the need to go for your goals head on, and you may be quite ruthless at times in order to achieve the goals you set yourself. For example, perhaps you don't care whose feelings you hurt or who loses out by your drive to get to the top of the ladder. However, this year, by learning to do things and treat people in a caring way, you may find that your path to success becomes easier as a result of the positive energy you put into life.

In a 1 Personal Year you may feel full of your own self-importance and feel superior to others. This is because with a 1 you may see yourself as the only one, or the one and only; this superior attitude may not make you popular with any colleagues. As an example, you may work in advertising and win a top contract from a major client as a result of your brilliant ideas. You may get so big-headed that you think people should bow down to you, or you talk down to people as if they were beneath you. Your work colleagues may put up with this for a short time if this is not your usual behaviour but they may become disenchanted if you continue, and in future end up walking the other way when they see you coming. However, it is wonderful to be able to use your creative gifts and to be good at your job, particularly during this 1 year cycle. But it may help you to be aware that everyone has their own gifts, and that you are not so different after all.

The number 1 highlights individuality and this may be evident in your life if you already have a number 1 in your chart. However, during this Personal Year you may find that you like to do things in your own unique way; for instance, perhaps you set up your own company and work for yourself during a 1 year (1 highlights independence). Perhaps you notice that people with strong individuality are attracted to work for you, or that the products you sell or your business has a streak of individuality about it. The influence of the 1 means that you may enjoy standing out from the crowd and leading others.

Paradoxically, you may be fearful of being your own individual, and you may withdraw even further from your work – if, say, you are called upon to assert yourself and stand out from the crowd. Sometimes, during a 1 Personal Year you may prefer to take up work where you can blend in to your work environment, even though you may be still making an excellent contribution to its success.

During a 1 Personal Year you may become more inventive about your work and you may be stimulated to try new ways to make your work more enjoyable, easier to do, or bring in different aspects which can make you more successful in your career.

With a 1 influencing you this year you may choose to work as a careers adviser, a researcher, a politician, a creative writer, or someone who takes a leading role within an organization or country. You may prefer to work on your own, or within a buzzy environment with lots of energy, vitality and chatter.

PERSONAL YEAR
2

You have been through a 1 Personal Year and in terms of your career you may have taken up new opportunities or set yourself new goals during this last year. Perhaps you are in a position of having lost your job or you have experienced a change of focus or direction with your career during this last year too. In which case during this 2 cycle you may find that your working life begins to balance itself out. For example, perhaps you find (new) work or a different career which fits in to balance with the whole of your life too. At the beginning of this 2 year cycle, the 1 energy is still influencing you to a degree. As a result you may sometimes find that your career goes into disharmony for a time while you are in the process of moving on with your career, finding your direction and finding your feet.

If during the 1 year cycle you have been working with one of its attributes – independence – and you have been working on your own, or for yourself, you may feel influenced to set up collaborative working relationships. This is because the 2 highlights sharing. For example, you way wish to share your workload, particularly if you found that you took too much work on for yourself during the 1 cycle. Or you may wish to employ a partner in your firm to share ideas, share the creativity and output and share the profits too. Perhaps you simply like the idea of having someone else as part of your team so that you can both work together towards your goals, and bounce ideas off each other. Sharing the workload can also help to make your life easier because when one of you is down, ill, on holiday, or at a meeting, there is still someone to carry on with the focus and goals.

Of course, you may have to learn to share and let some-one else take decisions as well as you, and if you are not used to this then it can take you time. Joint decision-making has its strengths, because if you both agree, for example, on the perfect name for your new product, then it can enable both of you to feel more confident about it (confidence is a 3 quality, a little of which is contained within the number 2). Sometimes allowing others to make important decisions with you may not be easy, particularly if you have been the only one making decisions for a long time. However, the more you learn to share the easier it becomes, and it can eventually seem like a completely natural process. Sharing may also involve sharing the workload, which may bring more productivity and creative output.

Decision-making is one of the key qualities that the number 2 highlights, and sometimes you may find that you are in situations where you have no choice about who you share your working life with. Your boss, for example, may have chosen the person who sits at the desk next to you, or the co-worker with whom you need to speak regularly in order for you to be able to carry out your job. However, you can decide whether you wish to work for your company, for yourself, and what work you do. If you are not happy at work you can choose to speak to those people directly and share your feelings with them, or about what you would like to do. You can also share with them when you are feeling happy and are enjoying your work so that this radiates out to them too.

The number 2 influences the emotions and if you are moody and unhappy within yourself it can really influence your creative output at work. And if you find yourself sat next to even one moody person this can influence your whole day. Of course you have the choice to remain happy and positive even when those around you are emotional. Your happy mood can make a positive contribution towards everyone's work output because it may help them to feel happy being around you.

During a 2 Personal Year you are also working to balance your emotions. Therefore, before you make any decisions about what work to take on, you may spend time deciding whether it can contribute towards creating harmony in your life.

With a 2 influencing you, particularly if you have a 2 in your chart already, you can find that your emotions make you feel as though you are on a merry-go-round – up and down. One minute you may love your job, the next minute you dislike it. Paradoxically, you can also find that the 2 provides a steady and stabilizing influence over your working life. Indeed you may also feel that this year your work gets too quiet and calm and that you become bored with your job. As an example, perhaps your company sells products that are seasonal and therefore the quiet times are even more challenging.

With the 2 influencing your work you may be challenged to find integrity and honesty within your working life. Perhaps you don't think that taking a writing pad from your desk home with you is dishonest because others do the same in the company. Or you may put down on your timesheet that you worked more hours in a week than you actually did (perhaps you arrive at work late many times but slip in through the back door so that nobody notices you). Integrity means being true to yourself, and when you are being dishonest nobody may ever find out, but *you* know, and you have to live with yourself. Most people tell little 'white lies' at times, but these can get out of hand, and you may eventually find it more and more difficult to be honest (even with yourself), particularly during this 2 Personal Year cycle.

Everyone has a shadow side which contains negative or challenging aspects or qualities which you are learning to transform. However, by being honest you tend to attract honest people to you, which can be much more rewarding at work (particularly where finances are concerned). Because honest working relationships help to bring in more productivity as you feel at ease with yourself, they can help you to be more successful from all the input of positive energy. During this 2 year cycle, by opening up to yourself, and being honest with yourself, it can help you to be calmer and to balance your emotions too.

You may be more closed off emotionally towards your workmates at times. This may be because the 2 influences vulnerability and you may feel too open and sensitive, and feel the need to cover yourself up and to hide your feelings from those you work with in order to try to protect yourself. Perhaps you become more insular (influenced by a little of the 3 energy contained in the number 2), or you may only feel safe to open up emotionally at home or with your friends, or your partner. You may also feel that you do not need to open up on this level to your work colleagues, which is your choice.

However, during a 2 Personal Year, when you cut your feelings off from certain people it can take up lots of energy. By allowing yourself to feel your feelings, even if you don't share them with those at work, you are freeing up your energy instead of pushing it down. When your energy is flowing at work it helps to bring balance to your whole life.

During a 2 cycle, you may be influenced to take up a career in the litigation field where you will be called upon to use your decision-making powers. You may also train or work as a nurse, a doctor, or as a therapist, where you can help others to feel well or help them to deal with their feelings. This can also help you to learn to relate to people on an emotional level.

PERSONAL YEAR

3

In a 3 Personal Year you are influenced a little by the 2 energy and the 4 energy contained within this number. Therefore, in relation to your career you are working to bring in emotional harmony (a 2 quality) and grounding (a 4 quality) to all areas.

Number 3 highlights a moving out into the world. Therefore you may wish to travel for or with your company to new destinations, or to open up another branch of your company in another part of town, or even in another country. Perhaps you look at ways of expanding your collection, if you are a fashion designer, for example, or if you are a chef you may expand by introducing new recipes.

In an ideal world, when you expand your thoughts, ideas and work into other areas, it is helpful to do it from a solid base or structure to give you firm roots to build from. Again a little of the 4 energy contained within 3 highlights these solid qualities. However, if your roots are not firm, for example, if you haven't done your research about a job you have been promoted into, or you start a new company selling products without researching the market first, then your attempts may be willowy and dissipate. Perhaps some of the roots catch hold and grow but others may simple fade away. Similarly, if you try to expand your company, or move into a new job too soon, your attempts may be less productive or even flounder. Expansion takes place all the time because life is constantly changing and moving on.

Within a 3 year you may be confident enough to fly through your career and find your success simply grows and grows. Perhaps this is simply because you have learned to go with the flow and allow life to carry you along while still offering positive input. Perhaps this year you earn an abundance of money, or perhaps you have an abundance of fun.

You have come through a 1 Personal Year when you may have needed to find a new direction in your career and a 2 year which may have taught you more about relating to people at work. During this year a light energy is brought in, encouraging a sense of humour, which can certainly help to get you through your working day. Perhaps you feel that this year there are so many things for you to handle that telling jokes, pulling funny faces, imitating people, or playing practical jokes on all and sundry is a good way for you to let your hair down. Or you are even the butt of someone else's practical jokes, which leaves you grinning from ear to ear. This 3 energy can really help to lighten any scene.

However, it may be that your boss or a client does not view your humour in quite the same way. Perhaps they think you are not serious enough about your work. This may well be the case during this 3 cycle, particularly if you are paying more attention to socializing than getting down to some hard work. Therefore it may help you to be aware that good work projects or jobs can slip through your fingers if you do not focus some of your energy their way.

Marcus works in advertising and in his Personal Year 3 his wife is expecting a child. He is preoccupied with worrying about her and that she is all right, and spends so much time popping home and ringing her that his clients notice and make a complaint. At this stage he realizes that he needs to let nature take its course, and decides to focus while he is at work.

Number 3 brings in the quality of superficiality and, like many television presenters, you can really get to grips with being all bubbly and light, fun and entertaining. However, superficial mistakes with your work, like sending the wrong letter to the wrong person, or failing to book the conference room for an important meeting, may be more important than you think. Indeed your boss or clients may overlook a few errors but constant misguided actions may cost you your job eventually.

Sometimes, as the result of the influence of the 3, at work you may find that you can do lots of different things at once and be confident about what you are doing. This is very helpful as you may achieve a lot more by the end of the day and your work colleagues may be duly impressed with the tasks you perform with such ease. However, if you look more closely you may find that yes you did a lot but did all of them superficially. For example, perhaps the report which needed to be handed in wasn't quite as detailed or long as it could have been, or the coffee you made for your colleagues was only lukewarm because you forgot about it while you were focusing on another job at the same time. Therefore during a 3 year it may be helpful to learn to prioritize the most important tasks to do each day; perhaps your morning cup of coffee is one of them!

With the influence of the 3 in your career this year you may be aware of extra criticism which seems to be flying around and aimed particularly at you. Perhaps it feels like people are picking on you or that whatever work you do it just isn't good enough. Sometimes people criticize your work because they instinctively pick up on your self-doubts, or lack of self-confidence about your work or yourself. Perhaps you also criticize their work too. During a 3 Personal Year if you are so good at giving yourself critical evaluation then others may like to join in and do it for you too. In this 3 cycle you may find it beneficial to take criticism with a pinch of salt and to learn to laugh and let things go. However, if the criticism is constructive then listening and taking note of ways in which you can improve your work productivity may really be of practical help.

The number 3 energy means that your career or work may expand at a great rate of knots with no time hardly to eat, sleep or think. Perhaps this is due to you putting in lots of energy and is the result of much activity aimed towards your goals. You may find this richly rewarding or you may not even have time to contemplate what it all means. However, the 3 also highlights the need for stillness. Taking time off (even a short time) to reflect on your work contribution and on the way your life is leading you forward may help to centre you. This can help you become even more focused on the most important issues within your work or career.

During a 3 Personal Year you may find that your career branches off into many different avenues, or that there are lots of new directions open to you. For example, you may be asked to become a professional singer because you have a wonderful voice, or someone else may ask you to set up a beauty company with them, and your current boss may also want to promote you, and so on. Sometimes lots of different leads all find their way to your door at once and your biggest challenge may be making a choice (a 2 quality influencing this 3 cycle) about which work to take on. However, during this year you may even be capable of trying many of them and then deciding which career path to take and to consolidate in your next 4 year cycle. With a 3 you may be a popular person as a result of your many talents and gifts, and this can also help to bring in an abundance of money for you.

You may find that this year is a time for expressing all your creativity. Perhaps you can take up drawing, painting, cooking, writing, playing a musical instrument, and so on. You may even decide to take up a (new) career in one of these areas. The number 3 may also bring out intellectual interests so you study to be a mastermind or work on some creative project which requires brain power too.

Even if you spend the year scattered and not knowing what to do next, then at least you can work with the uplifting energy of the 3 and be influenced by humour if you so choose.

PERSONAL YEAR
4

You are currently influenced by the number 4 within this Personal Year and this is a time to learn to materialize goals which you may have set yourself in previous cycles, particularly during the 1 year cycle. Where you may have been scattered and unable to focus all your attentions on your goals in your last cycle (year 3), during this year you can utilize the grounding influence of the 4 energy to give them clout. For example, you are an artist and during the last 3 year you were so busy designing so many different ranges of clothes, cards, cutlery and so on that you didn't have the time or energy to sell all these ideas to a manufacturer. Perhaps you only managed to sell one range, which was great in itself. However, the 4 energy helps to bring these ideas down to earth and literally ground them and perhaps you find that with even a little effort you may sell all your ideas to manufacturers.

When you are working within the confines of this 4 energy it is good to be aware that life is asking you to take one step at a time. This means taking each day as it comes and beavering away with your projects, ideas, or your work in order to achieve your goals. Sometimes with a 4 you may enjoy the process of 'chipping away at the wood' so much that you become indifferent to whether you achieve your goals or not. For example, if you are an accountant you may love working out all the facts and figures each day for your client, and this job satisfaction may be more important to you than any pot of gold.

Sometimes, in a 4 year you may decide to jump into things feet first (the 4 is influenced a little by the number 5 quality of spontaneity) and if you do then you may also find that the 4 energy helps to slow you down enough to keep your feet on the ground. This can particularly be of service if you are someone who often races through life. This can help to make the process of handling your working life easier because working in a step-by-step process means you are working through things thoroughly and you do not miss out on any experiences which can contribute towards you achieving your goals.

As a result of being influenced by number 4 in your Personal Year you may find yourself feeling heavy and bogged down with the process of each career step you need to make. Perhaps it seems like it is taking so long to achieve your goals, or during this cycle you may feel like you are never going to achieve them. Sometimes perseverance (a 4 quality) is needed during this cycle, and when things don't seem to go the way you planned you can simply 'get up' and carry on with all the little steps which lead to bigger steps later on.

You may be very determined to make your career work for you, and this concentration on your goals means that you may indeed succeed. For example, you may be struggling with financial challenges within your company as a result of a drop in demand for the services you supply. However, with the 4 bringing in a practical streak you keep your feet on the ground and decide to market your services (a quality of the 5 energy within this number) to other prospective buyers. Your determination this year may see you through a 'sticky' patch and ensure your company's survival.

Sometimes, you may experience events in your working life which challenge your abilities to stay grounded. Perhaps the company you work for may go bankrupt, or you find yourself taking a drop in pay in order to keep your job. The work changes may even be dramatic, you may go into work to find you are made redundant and have 1 hour to clear out your desk and leave. Major challenges in life, particularly to your material survival, can help to ground you because they are asking you to find ways of carrying on with your life no matter what.

With the 4 energy influencing your career this year issues around your career and money may be heightened because the number 4 highlights the material levels of your life. This may bring out inner insecurities about your material survival, and you may feel the need, for example, to hold on to your job. Perhaps to compensate you decide to work longer hours this year to prove that you are worth your position, or take on extra responsibilities. Perhaps you say 'yes' to every little piece of work which comes your way because you fear that you have to take what you can because the work may go away.

However, within a 4 Personal Year, particularly if this number is in your chart already, you are being asked to work on your inner sense of security. That is, to feel comfortable and safe within yourself, and when you do then you can practically handle whatever life brings your way. Of course you may only feel inner security some of the time during this 4 cycle because it is a quality you are working on to strengthen.

The number 4 highlights the need to build a solid structure in your working life. This may mean that you structure the hours you work in order to obtain maximum benefits to your career, you may structure your working environment to suit your practical needs, or you may structure your finances to cover your material needs, and so on. By applying structure to your working day you may indeed be able to get more work done as everything is in its place. During this cycle it may particularly help you to work on structure because the 3 and 5 energies which are free-flowing and boundless (5 qualities contained within this number 4) are influencing your working life.

Perhaps during this 4 year you decide to restructure your working life by rearranging your office, or the way you carry out your work, or by changing the content of your job. Paradoxically, this 4 energy may mean that you become too rigid and try to box yourself in with all the structure you try to impose.

The 4 energy highlights the building process, so during this cycle you may decide to build upon the career you already have, or on building a completely new career. For example, if you own a successful estate agency, then you may decide to invest your money by building another property company, in order to build upon what you already have. Perhaps you work for a financial institution and you decide to leave and set up your own company to build upon the experiences you have gained.

Usually when a new building is needed the old one has to be taken down before you can build a new one. In the same way, you yourself may have to start from scratch on your career because otherwise your career may not develop in the best possible way. Therefore during this 4 year cycle you may find that your career flounders and wilts as part of building a (completely) new career. The deeper you plant your roots the more powerful the results may be in the long run.

You may be influenced to take up a career as an administrator or an organizer where you can work on structuring your own, and your work colleagues' lives. Perhaps you decide to work as a farmer or do something physical like making things or restructuring things with your hands. The 4 may influence you to find a company with whom you can build your career longterm, which can help you to feel secure.

During this 4 Personal Year you are laying down the foundations for your future, which starts right now.

PERSONAL YEAR
5

You have just come through a 4 Personal Year, which means that you may have been focusing on grounding, structuring or laying foundations for your career to materialize. So with this fast-moving 5 energy now influencing you, be prepared for more movement to take you forward with your career plans and to take you further into life. Of course movement may carry you along a different path from the one you wish to follow because life is never completely predictable. However, this is one of the benefits of being influenced by this 5 energy this year as it generally means the grass doesn't even get the chance to grow under your feet.

With the influence of the 5 you may find that during this cycle your life is in constant movement and you are frequently being kept on your toes at work. This may simply mean that the telephone keeps ringing all the time and keeps you busy, or that your workload increases, or that you have more organizing to do to keep everything running smoothly, and so on. If you are the type of person who likes structure (perhaps you have a 4 in your chart) then this year may be challenging for you because it can literally sweep you off your feet. However, if you like change then the movement of the 5 energy can stimulate you, in which case you may find your work very exciting indeed.

Life is constantly changing but with the 5 influencing your career during this Personal Year be prepared for unexpected events. This is because the 5 energy can be volatile and unpredictable; it is like the wind which blows gently along on its path, then suddenly meets a whirlwind, intertwines then goes on its way again. During a 5 year your working life may seem like a constant whirlwind, and keeping grounded (a little of the 4 energy is influencing this 5 cycle) can help you to keep some order in your life. This is particularly helpful if and when unexpected work situations do arise.

You may find that you are also very changeable as a result of this 5 energy influencing you at work. For example, perhaps you decide you need to go to Switzerland for a business meeting and you arrange this, only to find hours later that you have changed your mind because you want your meeting to be held in your office instead. Having cancelled the aeroplane tickets you realize that you need to go to Switzerland anyway to meet a friend, so you rearrange your meeting where it was originally. This can be infuriating for those around you as you chop and change, and it can lose you money and valuable business colleagues too. Indeed, during this cycle, it may help you to work out the facts and the logistics of your work schedule before making any firm plans or arrangements.

During a 5 Personal Year you may also feel like you are being messed around by others changing their minds too often and perhaps this prevents you from carrying out your job as you may not know at times exactly what to do. For example, if you are booking a courier to deliver an essential item to another country, and they keep ringing you and changing the time of pick-up, you may not be able to leave your desk and get on with your work. You may feel nervous about leaving the package with someone else to give to them because it is so essential, and you prefer to give the parcel to them directly. Even if the delivery company is having an unpredictable day (perhaps they are influenced by 5s today!), at the end of the day you may tell them 'You're fired!' Their lack of commitment may have caused you much wasting of time, great uncertainty, and possibly lost you business.

It is helpful to be aware that life is full of variables, and what decisions you take in your career right now can influence your career tomorrow. Therefore with the 5 as your Personal Year influence you may be more aware of working out the facts before committing yourself. For example, before taking on a specific task you may ask 'what, when, where, why and how' in order to find out the potential ins and outs before you start. Working with facts this year may prevent you from chopping and changing later on. You may become so addicted to working out the facts in your head that it takes you ages to make any firm decisions. However, the 5 also influences perception and it may well be that you are able to read between the lines more easily about situations at work, and find ways forward with your career.

During this 5 Personal Year, work commitments are highlighted. Perhaps you find yourself starting lots of different work projects and then suddenly giving them up through lack of commitment. You may even run away from a job out of sheer lack of mental stimulation and boredom. Perhaps you think other jobs hold more adventure and stimulation; in a 5 cycle you may indeed think that the 'grass is always greener on the other side'. It is also possible that during a 5 year you think that moving from job to job can take you further up the ladder as each one offers you the experiences you think you need to get on with your life. However, learning to follow through on your commitments can often demonstrate to prospective employers or clients that they can count on you to get the work done. Perhaps by choosing your work commitments carefully you can gain satisfaction and enjoyment from learning to finish what you have begun.

During this Personal Year 5 you may be constantly looking for bigger and better thrills at work. For example,
perhaps you become restless with the same old weekly staff
meetings and you suggest someone sings a song to inject a
bit of life into them. You may even be the one offering this
service too! However, sometimes you spring into spontaneous action and you may be surprised when you don't
always receive your desired results. With this 5 energy you
may be simply stunned by spontaneous changes made 'out
of the blue' to the content of your working day which are
imposed upon you.

During a 5 year cycle the need for communication is
highlighted and you may find it easier to communicate and
discuss things with people at work. This can help you to
express yourself, particularly if you have a 5 in your chart
already, and you have previously found this challenging.
Sometimes the 'right' words may come easily to you and at
other times you may be struggling for things to say.
However, with the unpredictable influence of the 5 you may
also blurt out all kinds of things without thinking and find
that you are making some apologies for your outbursts to
work colleagues at a later date. Indeed with the 5 influencing you you may be very outspoken in the way you
communicate this year. This can be a good thing, for example, at times when something needs to be said to 'clear the
air' or for a work situation to be clarified so that everyone
can move on in a positive way. However, it may help you to
think before you speak at times as well.

With the 5 influence you may decide to become a
dancer or a singer, a deejay, or perhaps you decide to
embark upon a career as a travel writer as you lust to go out
into the world in search of fun and adventure. Perhaps you
decide to study some languages this year too, which may

also eventually open up your avenues to work and travel in foreign lands.

Perhaps you spend your time this 5 year developing your scientific brain by studying relevant subject matter or you may even become a full-time scientist or scientific researcher. The communications field may also lure you during this cycle too.

PERSONAL YEAR
6

With a 6 energy influencing this Personal Year you may find that you are able to achieve a lot of personal pleasure from your work. For example, you may normally do your work simply because you need to earn money to survive. The 6 influence can help to bring the enjoyment back into your work, even when you are carrying out the most simple or difficult tasks. Sometimes you may find that the pleasure you receive back from people as the result of your creative input is rewarding too; they may be extra nice to you.

You may love to please people during this cycle and you may find it very challenging if your work doesn't bring a smile to the faces of your colleagues. For example, if you make some mistakes on a work project you may blame yourself if the project doesn't succeed, and you may feel really sensitive about it emotionally. Indeed, you may really take it to heart. Perhaps you try to make up for it by being extra attentive on your next work project, or by being extra nice to your work colleagues. You may also prefer to leave your job this year rather than continue to work with people who aren't pleasant, or who are darn right rude, unhelpful, or uncaring in their attitude. This is because you are extra sensitive with the 6 energy influencing you during this 6 cycle.

With the influence of the 6 energy you may find that you become more involved in team work or wish to work with groups. Perhaps you are used to working with a group of people, but if you aren't then this can bring in a whole new dimension to your working life. You may thrive off and love working with your team and you may find you can accomplish projects even more easily when you are all collectively focused on the same goals.

The number 6 also highlights group responsibilities and as part of the group you may be only too aware of what those are, and how you can contribute. In the 6 cycle you may really enjoy the support of working in a group, and the sensitive 6 energy may encourage you to be more aware of other people's needs too. Perhaps you notice that one of your work colleagues is struggling with a piece of work so you give them emotional support to help them get through. Or when you notice a work deadline creeping close you offer to work extra hours in order to make sure the whole group meets its target on time.

During this year you may be extra caring towards your work colleagues but you may also find that you neglect your own work in order to help them out. Perhaps this means that you get into trouble with your boss for not completing your work, and that then you blame the other person for needing your help in the first place. You may even feel resentment towards them for causing you distress. Perhaps you even blame yourself for not paying enough attention to your own work.

However, during this cycle you are learning that before you can take responsibility for others and help others you also need to learn to take responsibility for yourself. Therefore any decisions you take are as a result of the choices you have made. During this cycle, it may help you to make decisions which can benefit the whole group, and this includes you too. By loving and looking after your own needs at work it can benefit the whole team, or the whole project you are working on.

In a 6 Personal Year the quality of service is highlighted. Being of service means that you learn to give to others what they need, and during this cycle learning to step aside and see others' needs may be what you are required to do. This may be challenging for you, particularly if you can be selfish and feel that the whole world is there simply to serve you. You may work in a shop and enjoy serving customers all day long and seeing the pleasure on their faces when they buy something they want. Perhaps you work for an airline and you serve customers as a steward/ess on a business journey across the world. You may also be in service to your employees if you own a (large) organization by giving lots of people employment and a wage at the end of the day. Service comes in many forms, and you can even serve your work colleagues by giving them a smile, and a polite salutation when you see them too.

In a 6 Personal Year you may be so aware of service that you take on much more work than you can handle and you may bow under the strain, particularly emotionally. Perhaps you feel angry with yourself because you feel put upon by your boss or your work colleagues. However, in a 6 year you are learning to serve yourself too because if you are too tired to perform to the best of your abilities then you are of no use to anyone. By learning to say no to work when you feel you have enough already can help you to give to everyone in a positive way.

Sometimes in a 6 cycle you can get your teeth stuck into your work and go on and on and on with it, until you have no energy left for anything else. Perhaps you become obsessive with your work and with your creative output. You may find that some of your emotions are tied up in your work too and that you really feel the need for it to go well. Getting carried away with your work means that when you do eventually finish it you may not feel the need to repeat that kind of work again. And you will have learned a great deal about your own emotions, and your work capacity too. With a 6 influencing you you may really enjoy going deeply into your work.

The 6 energy is influencing you this year, which means that commitments at home may take precedence over commitments at work. This is because 6 influences family issues, which may arise during this year. Of course you can choose to work from home, which may be a preferable way to balance out your work and home life. With a little of the 5 energy contained within this 6 you may find making commitments a challenge, particularly ones which can affect whole groups of people, which include work and family groups too. Perhaps you shy away from work commitments in order to preserve your family life in some way.

With the influence of a 6 you may be preoccupied with perfection and getting your work right. Perhaps you keep working on the same document for an important presentation until it is precisely the way you want it. Your high ideals may also mean that you drive your employees or work colleagues on and on to perfection too. Sometimes, learning to let go when you feel that something is not quite perfect may mean that you learn to accept life the way it is.

This year you may take up work within your local community, perhaps as a social worker, or as a carer, or even as a legal representative who looks after the welfare of the community. Perhaps you take up work as a photographer, painter and decorator, or as a fashion or clothes designer. You may like to feel good and feel au fait with the people you work with because looks alone may not guarantee that you stay in a job during this 6 Personal Year.

7

You are currently influenced by a 7 cycle which means that you have the opportunity to capitalize on the efforts you have put into your career during the last 6 Personal Years. For example, in your last 1 Personal Year the idea may have popped into your head that you would like to be a pilot and you may have enquired about training. In your 2 year you may have weighed up whether you would really like to move careers and considered the information about the training. In your 3 cycle perhaps you embarked upon the flight training course learning 'theory', and during your 4th Personal Year consolidated this by flying an aeroplane (although in tandem with an instructor). During your 5th cycle (which emphasizes movement and travel) you may have been really keen on flying and practised a lot. During your 6 Personal Year you see how best you can serve yourself and others within your career. You pass your pilot's exams (with flying colours) in this current 7 Personal Year cycle, and you may leave your old career behind. This is one potential case scenario.

This year there is a little of the 8 energy influencing your current cycle, therefore even when you do become a professional pilot you may still be re-evaluating (an 8 quality) if you are doing the right thing. Perhaps this year, while re-evaluating, you feel it may be a good idea to take some advanced pilot training.

Sometimes, you may miss out on any or many of the 6 stages leading up to this 7 Personal Year, in which case it may mean that you do not decide to become a pilot (perhaps you changed your mind in the 5 year cycle). Or perhaps you didn't pay enough attention to your theory studies in the 3 cycle because you much preferred the 'hands on' practice in your 4 Personal Year, for example. Therefore during this 7 year you may decide to take up another career instead, perhaps because you realize after tentatively approaching the idea of being a pilot that it isn't for you. Perhaps you fail one part of your exams and need to retake it during the 8 year cycle, and so on.

Within your cycles from 1 to 9 you may decide to begin a new career at any time, but each cycle contains strong energies which can influence how you will do this. For example, if you were to begin a new job or embark upon a new career during a 2 Personal Year then you may do it very gently, and the choice to change may be very simple for you. You may also start new projects or work during your 4 Personal Year, as a result of you restructuring your life on the physical level. Every day is an opportunity for change. But in this 7 year you can clearly see that your career materializes as a direct result of the choices you have made during each cycle, and from the amount of work you have put in.

The 7 energy influences your emotions and during this year you may be able to feel, through your gut instincts, exactly what you need to do in terms of your career. However, it is also necessary to use positive thoughts and a positive mind to help you too. During the 7 year you may find that what you think seems to materialize instantly, and this is one very good reason to be clear about your intentions. For example, you decide you would like to hold a conference meeting for all the employees in your company to give them some stimulating information about health-care. You may have the thought about this on Monday and three days later the talk goes ahead. Within that time you had spoken to the various departments involved, organized the time, venue, refreshments, speaker and cost, and your idea developed into the reality.

In a 7 year you may gain much satisfaction from being able to produce things out of thin air, and you may also find that when things don't (instantly) materialize you are very disappointed indeed. Sometimes you need to be aware, during this 7 year cycle, that the bigger cycles of life govern everyone and everything. So, for example, perhaps you may have done all you could to organize a wonderful talk but perhaps an emergency meeting meant many people couldn't attend, which was out of your hands.

During this cycle you may experience a very productive year at work. However, the 7 energy also means that you can be unrealistic about your work expectations, and dreamy. Perhaps you dream that a perfect job will float your way without your telling anyone that you are even looking for one. In your imagination you may also dream up the perfect career and think you can have it overnight. For example, you may dream that you'd like to be a ballet dancer even though at the age of twenty-one you've never had a lesson in your life. Of course miracles do happen (perhaps with a little influence of the 8 within this number 7, which influences karma, you were a ballerina in a past life!) and perhaps you can dance naturally.

However, in a 7 year you may be asked to 'get real' and to learn to walk before you can run ahead with your career. Indeed, if you are always dreaming about your ideal job then you may not be giving any attention to your current work which means less creativity and output during this 7 cycle. With this 7 energy influencing dreams then you may find you have psychic dreams (influenced by the 6 energy within this number) which show areas of work which may suit you. However, with the 7 highlighting a vivid imagination, working in the creative field where you need to think up wonderful ideas and be imaginative may be just up your street.

When you are positive and clear about what work you need to do during this 7 cycle then you may find that you get through it quickly. The number 7 highlights nature and when your work is flowing it is because you are aligned to your natural cycles and what you are meant to be working at. For example, if you are a diplomat, and you love your work so much because the job comes naturally to you, then during this 7 cycle perhaps you negotiate amazing peace deals between countries, or find some little miracles occur within your work. Miracles are laws of nature and therefore this year, by trusting the process of nature guiding you within your career, anything can happen.

Equally so, during this 7 Personal Year, you may be destructive in your working environment as a result of a lack of trust in the process of life. For example, perhaps you are told that you may lose your job this year. You think this is because you have been neglecting (an influence of the 6 energy in the 7) your work, as you have been paying more attention to your lover. You may become so downhearted and negative in thought and speech about your company that you may give them the final reason for asking you to leave. When you go into a downward spiral of doom and gloom within this 7 cycle then you may indeed end up with very little work indeed. However, by trusting the process of life you may eventually find that life leads you where you are meant to be. For example, leaving your company may mean that eventually you find new work which is much more interesting and ideal.

With the 7 influencing your career this year you may take up work as a researcher or perhaps you decide to research the line of work you are already involved in. Perhaps you become a film producer where you can literally see your creative input come together on the silver screen. You may also enjoy working with numbers this year, and perhaps you take up work as a numerologist or as an accountant.

During this 7 Personal Year you may find that you get the icing on the cake in terms of work, or that work simply slips through your fingers and disappears out of reach, with you simply being left to dream about it.

PERSONAL YEAR
8

You have worked your way through the 7 Personal Year cycles and during this year you are influenced by the 8 cycle. In numerology the 8 and 9 cycles are times to re-evaluate and to tie up loose ends from the previous 7 cycles.

You may find during this Personal Year that you appear to be going over old ground in terms of your work content, and you may even feel like you are regressing in terms of the progress of your career. For example, during your last 5 Personal Year you were learning about how to write a press release as you are a publicist. After 3 years of writing your own information during this cycle your employer may suggest you take some extra training because your style is not up to standards of expectation (a 9 quality, a little of which is contained within this cycle 8). Perhaps you reluctantly agree – you can be very stubborn with this 8 energy influencing you. It may appear that are being reprimanded, but in effect you have the opportunity to polish up your writing skills, and by revisiting and relearning even for a few hours it has given you valuable input into your work. Perhaps you become even more successful with your publicity material from now on.

Sometimes during an 8 Personal Year by going back you gain because you are picking up little pieces of information that you left behind which can help you with your current career or your future working life. However, you may not always want to revisit work situations, particularly if they were very challenging for you. For example, perhaps you were moved to a different department at work as a result of a boss who was always bearing down heavily on you with a heavy workload. For a time during the last 7 Personal Years you were happy to continue with your work for the same company. However, in this 8 year cycle you may turn up at work to find that your company has moved your old boss into your current department and you do not wish to relive your old working relationship again. However, you may find that your boss's attitude has changed, or that your attitude has changed too. Perhaps you have both learned to change your patterns of behaviour which were creating the situation between you. Therefore, although it may seem like you are going back this year it may be because you need to revisit situations in order to let them go and to move on with your life.

If you have number 8 in your chart already you may find that you get into your own personal power this year by asserting yourself at work. This may mean that you ask for a pay rise, ask for different working conditions, ask to be treated fairly (a quality of the 9 which influences the number 8 to a degree), and so on. If you do not normally find self-assertion easy then the 8 energy can help to bring this out of you.

Sometimes when you are learning to flex this muscle you may find it so difficult that your assertiveness actually manifests itself as aggressiveness. For example when you ask your boss for a pay rise you may be so fearful of a refusal, or of asking for your financial needs to be met, that you blurt it out in a loud aggressive voice. When you may have been wanting to ask in an authoritarian, cool and collected voice by asserting your viewpoint directly and powerfully. Learning to be assertive can take time, and in the meantime at least you managed to ask your boss for a pay rise, which may in itself be quite an achievement.

The number 8 is particularly associated with finance and you may find that money becomes an issue this year. For example, you may want more money and therefore work very hard to make this happen. Or you may find that you focus much of your time talking about how you are going to be rich, without doing anything practical about it. In which case you may be experiencing a little of the dreamy 7 quality influencing this 8 year. In an 8 Personal Year you may want to make money bigtime and to be so successful with your life that you never need to work again. However, you may also 'break your back' doing it, and with your eyes focused so strongly on your purse strings it may leave little enjoyment for anything else. This may include the work you actually do in order to secure your fortune.

Money can be a contentious issue and what appears to be the jackpot for one person is nothing to someone else. Indeed money in itself is nothing but energy, and it is how you handle this energy that determines whether you make money or not. For example, you may hold on to money for security and hoard it, even though you have no real use for extra disposable income within your current lifestyle. Depositing money into a bank account which doesn't move stagnates, and this psychologically is a mirror of your stagnating energy too. When your energy stagnates in one area it affects all the other areas of your life. Arguably your money in your bank account is energy which is usually being used and invested by your bank so it is circulating around the world in some way. However, you perceive it to be there in its exact amount, and that is what is important to you.

Mike is an engineer who works all the hours which are sent him in order to secure a good wage and a pension for the future. He has worked for the company for sixteen years and in this Personal Year 8 he hears that he is to be made redundant. He decides to embark upon a completely new career which is not paid abundantly but which means that he works fewer hours and is richly rewarded spiritually.

In this 8 year be aware if you let your energy flow by receiving and spend money in equal amounts according to your necessity. Or whether you hold on to your energy (and money) and therefore prevent it from flowing and bringing you in even more financial gain which can be used in a productive way. Making money is great, particularly when you can enjoy it at the end of the day, or even better still enjoy it with others.

The 8 energy contains a spiritual and a physical element and therefore during this Personal Year cycle it may help you to learn to balance these aspects in your working life. For example, perhaps you love earning money, you also love the colleagues you work with (you feel spiritually connected to them), and you love the work that you do too. When these areas of your life are all taken care of during this 8 cycle you may find out what it is to have true success in your working life.

With the 8 influencing you this year you may be inclined to bully your way to success, by bullying customers, staff, your bank manager, and anyone who finds themselves on your path. Perhaps you think this is your right because you think you have something (a product to sell, for example) which nobody else has got and you bully them into giving you what you want. In this 8 Personal Year, the law of karma rules, not you, which means that what you give out to others you get back, and life may deliver you a few orders not on your demanding list, like another bully, or someone who may just put you out of business or teach you a long-earned karmic lesson.

The 8 energy highlights responsibility and is asking you to learn to stand on your own feet and take responsibility for your behaviour too. Indeed, you can be extra charming during this cycle, particularly with an 8 in your chart already, and although you can be manipulative too, being charming is a more positive way to go about *getting* what you want.

With the influence of the 8 Personal Year you may choose to work with money, for example, as a book-keeper, an accountant, a financial director, a shop-keeper, or as an administrator. Perhaps you use your assertiveness to take charge of a project, or become a boss or the owner of your own company.

The 8 energy brings in the quality of 'will' and you may find your will to succeed drives you on this year in whatever career or work you choose to do.

PERSONAL YEAR
9

In this 9 Personal Year you are transforming from the last 9 year cycle into a new 9 year cycle (which begins in the 1 Personal Year) and therefore this cycle influences endings and new beginnings. Sometimes when you are going through transformation it does not always feel comfortable, even if in this case your career prospects are better when you come out of the other end.

Indeed, each day is a complete transformation from the dark to the light of day, and back to darkness again, and at each turn you learn more about life. However, sometimes you cannot see the light for the darkness which shadows you and therefore during this 9 Personal Year you may feel a loss of faith in your work abilities or in your career. Perhaps it doesn't seem to be working out in quite the way you expected (the 9 influences high ideals), or perhaps it feels that nothing is happening at all. When you go through quiet times and can't seem to concentrate on your work it may be because there are so many inner changes going on. Perhaps you find that when you need to work out some really important work issue for yourself then you create the outer space to do this. These are potential times for great transformation and it may be that your career really moves forwards fast after one of these inward journeys.

During this 9 cycle you may find that you need to use your mind to discriminate about what you would like to let go of and move forward with into your next 9 year cycle. For example, if during your last Personal Year 6 you learned to work with a whole team of people (instead of working by yourself in the main) then you may discriminate about

how this can work practically in your current or prospective career. That is, if you are intending to become
self-employed during this 9 or your next 1 Personal Year
cycle you may wonder how you can incorporate teamwork
into this – particularly if you enjoyed working as part of a
group immensely. By making decisions about what work
you intend to do now it can help you to move on with a
clear focus into your new 1 year cycle.

At times during this 9 cycle when you use your logical
brain to discriminate about things then you may find that
you base your decisions on what you think is 'right' or
'wrong'. You may also be swayed by what others think is the
right thing for you to do too. For example, you may wish to
write a book about the environment because you think this
is the 'right' thing to do, but your friends and family may
tell you that your time is better used by writing a book on
music or cookery instead. They may say this because you are
a professional musician or chef already and they see this as
the logical and 'right' thing for you to do next. With a 9
influencing you during this Personal Year you may find that
listening to your own inner guidance, in addition to using
your logical brain, can help you to make the best possible
career choices.

You are influenced by a 9, therefore power issues may
arise this year. Perhaps you are the powerful leader of a company and you take this responsibility seriously by handling
the power at your command carefully and wisely and for
everyone's benefit. Perhaps this 'right' handling of power
means that others bestow even more power on you by offering you further career responsibilities. Power is simply an
energy, and during this 9 Personal Year you can see how it
weaves its way through your career path. For example, you
may be promoted to a managerial position and discover your

love for power makes you a dictatorial leader (an 8 quality which influences the 9). You may even have power clashes with your work colleagues too. Perhaps you think you *are* the power, and forget that the promotion to manager, the power which came your way, was from a higher source outside of you. By aligning to the energy of power which is influencing your career this year and working with this energy, instead of going on power trips and thinking you *are it*, you may become an even more powerful person.

However, you do not need to be a managing director or hold a high rank to be a powerful person. Power shines through your work when you are simply being you, and getting on with your career in the best way you can. Being yourself at work is the most powerful gift you can give to the world, and one which can empower everyone around you to be powerful by being themselves too.

One way you can lose any delusions of grandeur during this 9 year cycle and become more powerful is by being of service to your work colleagues. As an example, perhaps you are a teacher and you are so devoted to helping your pupils to be educated, and for the school to do well, that you forget yourself as you work towards these goals (a 1 quality, a little of which influences this 9 Year). Indeed the 9 highlights compassion and selflessness, and particularly if this number is in your chart already, you may lead others by the good example you set this year.

With the influencing of a 9 you may become very pious and preach to people about certain ways in which you would like their work to be carried out. You may even reprimand those who try to cross your path or who rebel against your commands. Indeed you may hold them in the most utmost contempt. 'How dare they carry out that task any other way!' you may say. Sometimes this is because you have such high work standards and high work ethics too. You may be very keen on good behaviour at work, and politeness and manners may be among your basic demands for any employee or employer who works with you during this 9 cycle.

Paradoxically, this year may bring out the rebellious side in you too, and at work you may refuse to budge. For example, you may think you know the 'right' way for a document to be presented and no matter what your boss says you present it your way. Or you discriminate about which are the important telephone calls to make in any one day, even though your boss requests otherwise. However, being rebellious and being conformist are both elements contained within the 9 energy; you may experience both aspects to some degree within your working life this year.

You may decide to get involved with work politics this year. Perhaps you give a speech to your work colleagues about ways in which you think the company or work situations can be improved. Or you may even start a weekly debate at work so that everyone can air their views on company policies. You may even earn yourself the title of troublemaker as you are unafraid to confront even the toughest work issues, in order for the whole company to benefit. You may show great inner strength when tackling these issues. Perhaps some of the topics you raise are to do with environmental politics, food politics, lifestyle politics, all of which may be associated with the way the company carries out its daily routine. During this 9 cycle you may even be inspired to extend your interest in these topics further and become a professional environmentalist, or politician.

The 9 can influence you by providing you with a keen sense of justice so that you do not simply get on your hobby horse for the sake of it, or to ruffle people up the wrong way, but in order to show others a better way of living.

You may also find that you are influenced by the casual, relaxed and liberal energies encouraged by the 9 cycle. Perhaps you spend your time learning to play the guitar so that you can play in a band, or so that you bring some relaxation into your working life during this last year of your current 9 year cycle.

3

PERSONAL YEARS AND YOUR LIFE AT HOME

'Home is where your heart is' it is said, in which case your home is literally your physical body, but it is also the place in which you eat, sleep, and live also. Your home is one of the most important aspects of your life because it provides you with a base from which to go out into the world. Indeed if you found stability at home during your childhood, particularly during the first 7 years of your life, then this can also have a stabilizing influence over your whole life.

Within the Personal Year cycles you can observe the kind of changes which may take place at home, within your physical environment, and within your relationship to your home and those living in it. Each cycle brings out an emphasis on different energies which are influencing that specific Personal Year.

Your home environment is influenced by the collective energies which are attributed to the Universal Year which you are in. For example, the year 2013 adds up to a 6, and 6 highlights love and compassion, so even if you are personally experiencing disruptions at home it may be made easier by the warmth of this universal collective 6 energy. However, you may also lack compassion, in which case life at home may be even more challenging at times during 2013.

By observing the greater universal cycles it can help you to realize what energies and qualities all your family members, or those who live at home with you, may be experiencing during this cycle. Your own Personal Year cycles highlight specific potential experiences which are relevant to your home life during each cycle too.

1

You have come through a 9 year cycle and so you may be ready to move forward into a whole new environment at home and in yourself. For example, you may wish to move house or home during this cycle to go for a complete new beginning, or you may simply turn your home upside down by decorating it from top to bottom. The 1 brings in the potential of new energy, and you may find within yourself incredible amounts of energy which drive you forward to change your environment this year.

Sometimes, decorating and changing around objects in your home can give you more energy as it stimulates your mind, body and spirit. You may even find that by simply moving a little furniture around, hanging a new picture on the wall, or changing the colour of a tablecloth and so on, it can really boost your energies.

With the 1 as a Personal Year influencing your mind, you may find that your mental attitude towards your home is key to your happiness during this cycle. For example, you may be very angry with one specific person you are living with, or even at the presence of your cat or dog, and this attitude can have a negative influence over your physical environment. Perhaps you feel frustrated with the way your home is decorated and perhaps you don't have the time, energy or inclination to change it.

With the 1 energy influencing your home life you may find that objects around your home appear to break down easily and it may even seem at times like nothing actually works. For example, the picture on the television screen goes all fuzzy (as a result of outside electrical disturbances), or the washing machine gets stuck on a rinse and won't empty, and so on. Everything may even seem to break down at once.

Destruction is a natural part of the moving forward process and this quality is contained within the cycle number 1. Sometimes things need to break down before new things can replace them or before they can be mended. When things break down you get the opportunity to examine why it has happened. For example, perhaps the pipe is blocked up with gunge from the washing machine, or perhaps you left the aerial out of the television, and so on. Then you can do something about it.

However, the number 1 influences the ability to solve practical problems and to come up with wonderful ideas which can help make your life at home go smoother during this cycle. This is again because the logical mind is activated by the 1 energy and even if you are normally hopeless at brainstorming ideas, this year you may excel!

With this 1 mirroring your personal life at home you may find situations break down to some degree this year because the 1 moves through your life with a forceful energy. This may mean that you have challenges relating (a 2 energy which influences the 1 a little) to your family or people who live with you. Perhaps as a result of this 1 energy you feel more withdrawn from those around you too, or you may feel like they are withdrawing from you too at times.

Sometimes when changes occur in your home environment or when you are going through deep inner changes which move you forward with your life, you may need to withdraw into yourself for a while. Withdrawing mentally from the world means that you give yourself the space to work out in your mind exactly what you would like to do next. You may withdraw mentally by refusing to think about problems and by focusing your attention on something else. For example, if you have a major challenge with work which is very busy at the moment then you may refuse to think up ways in which you can better the situation and when you come home you may wish to think of or discuss anything but that subject. Alternatively, if it is your situation at home which is causing a concern then you may switch off from it whilst you are there and think of your work instead.

It may also be that your life moves forward with great speed during this 1 Personal Year cycle and you may feel the need to withdraw into your own room at home for a while, perhaps for a few hours. With a little of the 2 energy influencing this 1 cycle then one of its qualities, calmness, can be applied to help relieve the pressures of adapting to new people or situations when life seems to be whizzing by.

The 1 cycle highlights new opportunities, but it is up to you whether to go for them, and if you don't during this 1 year then you may 'miss the boat'. Yes, some opportunities do return, but others only happen once in your lifetime. For example, you see a dream home which you and your partner fall in love with, but because you deliberate about the price for too long and fail to put in an offer it's too late. The 1 energy is influencing you to move forward in a positive way and to really go for what you want in life, which includes your home.

During a 1 Personal Year you may find that you have more direction with your life in general and therefore you may have more energy to put into your relationships at home. For example, the 1 influences new beginnings and you may find that your relationships with those you live with move forward in a new and different way this year as a result of a fresh input.

The 1 highlights the need to move ahead with your life and if you have been involved in situations at home where you felt you were unable to move forward then the 1 energy can help. Of course you may not always like the direction life leads you in. The number 1 highlights the power of the mind or the 'will' and during this Personal Year sometimes the greater collective 'will' decides exactly what is best for you. For example, you may decide to paint your bedroom orange, and take a day off work to do this. However, you find that your local paint shop has run out of the colour orange so you end up taking the next best which is yellow instead. You paint your bedroom and are relieved that it looks superb, and glad that the higher powers sorted out the best possible colour for you.

With a 1 in your Personal Year, particularly if you have this number in your chart already, then you may prefer to keep your home really intimate and to allow only those who are close to you to come in through its doors. This may be because you fear people getting too close to you, or because you are a very private person. Perhaps you make the decoration really intimate and personal to your taste too. The 1 cycle can influence you to open up and let new people into your home, and perhaps to form a new home situation with other people.

Ambition is highlighted within this 1 energy, therefore you may set yourself tasks to bring out this quality. For example, you may like your whole family to move out of your home to temporary accommodation while it is being completely redecorated. However, you may be over-ambitious with your ideas and find that some of them don't work; hence your temporary home becomes a more permanent home for longer than you thought.

With the 1's influence you may be more independent during this Personal Year cycle and want to be creative and do any DIY around the home by yourself. You may get great satisfaction from achieving some positive results. Perhaps you decide to live alone this year to learn about independence, and at other times you may feel that you really need to have an independent life outside your (family) home.

During this 1 cycle the old patterns are breaking down and making room for new experiences in your home life.

PERSONAL YEAR
2

During a 2 Personal Year you are influenced by your emotions and therefore these may come into play with regard to any decisions you make about your home life. It may be that your head has been ruling you during your last Personal Year 1 (1 is associated with the mind), and therefore moving into this 2 energy may feel like a shock. Perhaps you find that little things people do around the home upset you easily, like forgetting to put the top on the toothpaste or scrunching up your newly ironed clothes by placing a book on top of them, and so on.

With this 2 energy you may feel very vulnerable and sensitive indeed to the people you live with, or to your neighbours, particularly ones who seem to be selfish about their own needs. For example, your neighbour may leave their garbage strewn in front of their front door so that everyone who comes into your home sees it. This does not bring in a nice ambience to your living environment, and you may diplomatically ask them to remove it. You may find out that your neighbours weren't even aware of their actions, or they may have just been insensitive to your needs. With this strong 2 energy influencing you, you may even get emotional with them if they refuse your request.

The 2 highlights your potential to be able to see other people's points of view. You may make special efforts to weigh up your own needs and those of people you live with. For example, perhaps you would like to host a family dinner party on Sunday evening and your boyfriend wants his friends to come over as well. By being able to recognize both your needs you may resolve this situation by joining both groups of people together, or having both friends and family around at different times on Sunday instead. Then both of you can enjoy your lovely home together.

During a 2 Personal Year you may notice the emotions of people you live with more. For example, perhaps you notice that your wife or husband is very sensitive to remarks about their cooking. Maybe you hadn't realized that your comments touched any sore points, or went in deeper than just an observation (which is the way you viewed it). This year, if you find that you are opening up to your own emotions and being open to life generally, then you may suddenly be more aware of others' feelings at home. Sometimes, particularly if you have been shut off from your emotions towards people you live with then this 2 energy can help you to open up and get closer to them emotionally.

With emotions highlighted during this 2 cycle you may find yourself very emotional at home and you may contribute towards creating a heavy atmosphere in your environment. If you live with people who are sensitive already then they may find your moods or emotions challenging at times. Perhaps visitors to your home also notice this and feel uncomfortable or ill at ease at times. However, life is a balancing act and this 2 energy can help to balance your emotions, and bring into your home a calming influence which can help everyone who lives with you.

During this 2 Personal Year you may decide to make simple changes to your home. For example, you may decorate it with simple furnishings, perhaps with one colour or one style, or bring in a few furnishings which can make all the difference to the atmosphere, and so on. If you live with someone else you may have to take into consideration their feelings about any changes in the colour scheme. During this cycle you are learning to feel what is best for everyone in your home.

If you are feeling emotional during this 2 Personal Year you may become extra sensitive to the colours around you at home. For example, if you have lots of blues and greens in your home (which look watery) this may encourage you to feel watery and emotional. This is because watery colours can remind you of the sea and your inner emotions. However, some deep blues and greens may help to have a calming effect on you. You may feel like experimenting with colour during this cycle to find the best possible colours to help balance your emotions out.

Mary works as an interior designer so she is particularly aware of the power of colours in the home. Having recently moved to a new home with her partner in this Personal Year 2, she decides to compromise on the decoration and to find colours which they both like so that they can both feel in harmony in their home.

With the 2 influencing your home life you may feel the need to invite lots of loving and caring people into your home, because the 2 highlights love and warmth. You may feel extra loving yourself and this love may exude out into your external environment too. You may also want to create a really caring and warm atmosphere and want it to feel harmonious. For example, perhaps you have lots of soft rugs littering the floor, comfy chairs which soothe you when you lounge in them, and crystals to bring in lots of light to your home. Perhaps you have many plants nurturing the environment too.

In a 2 year you may work on building harmonious relationships with those at home, which means that your physical environment may reflect this. For example, you may build a water feature in your living-room or a fish tank which can help to soothe you and keep you calm, or you may use peaceful music to add to the soothing atmosphere.

With a 2 energy influencing this cycle you may find that your home loses its sense of tranquillity as a result of your emotional outbursts. Perhaps, particularly if you have a 2 in your chart, you become confrontational and argumentative with those who visit you or live at home. You may also be touchy at times and defensive, which means finding peace in your home life may be difficult for those around you. Everyone has their moods, but in this 2 year, by opening up and trying to relate to those around you it may help to create a more peaceful space to live in for everyone.

The 2 energy means that your home situation can feel unbalanced at times this year. This may be because you feel like you are always giving emotionally, as you sit around listening to everyone's problems. If you feel the need for help then you may need to ask for their support. Those at home may be only too willing to help you if you ask. Paradoxically, with a 2 in your chart during this 2 cycle you may find that you are the one people always give to at home, and perhaps it is your turn to learn to give. However, when you give you naturally receive on some level anyway, and vice versa.

This year you are learning to share yourself with others (a 2 quality) at home. In order to do this you need to be able to open to giving and receiving the good feelings and the challenging feelings too. For example, perhaps you and your lover feel sad because you have both lost a child, or you may feel happy because you have just got married and this is your first home. Sharing the good times and the not so good are two polarities of this 2 energy.

In this 2 Personal Year you are being asked to learn to find ways of cooperating with people at home in order to bring harmony into your life. To do this you need to find some degree of harmony within yourself first. Being selfish (a little of this 1 quality is influencing the 2) may be one way to focus on your own emotional needs. Then perhaps you can learn to open up your emotions to those you live with, and live with them in harmony.

PERSONAL YEAR

3

You have come through a 1 Personal Year of moving forward with your home life, a 2 year where you were working on finding harmony at home, and you are now influenced by a 3 in this cycle, which brings in the qualities of movement and expansion. Expansion may mean that you literally need to move into a bigger home, perhaps because you have been buying so many new things and there is nowhere to store everything. It may also mean that your current home is bursting at the seams as you try to store everything in it. Perhaps you become much more untidy during this year and find it difficult to place your hands on things when you need them as you forget where they are in the chaos. Perhaps your home life has people running in and out in all different directions and all for different reasons.

Indeed there may be so much movement during this cycle that you may not know what you are doing next. For example, perhaps you go to make some tea for your guests, answer a business call (you work from home), while trying to fit in opening your mail. It may well help you to bring in some of the balancing 2 energy (a little of which is contained within this 3) this year in order for you to fully function.

Sometimes, during this cycle you may find that the 3 energy brings in an incredible ability to cope with even more home activities. For example, you may normally find looking after your brother's two children, plus your own family, cats and dogs, impossible and you usually end up tired and exhausted at the end of the day. With this light 3 energy you may find that at times you are able to focus on all of them, and indeed you may feel uplifted by having them around.

The 3 highlights mental worries and may mean that during this Personal Year you quickly get bogged down with challenges at home. For example, if you find your mortgage payment didn't go through (by no fault of yours) you may worry until you feel ill. However, this 3 energy is encouraging you to keep your mind positive and to look on the bright side of life. Sometimes by letting in just a little sunshine when you are facing real challenges in your life you can get through, particularly during this 3 cycle.

With a 3 influencing this year you may like to lighten up your mind from worries and also literally lighten up your apartment or home. You may do this by painting bright sunshine colours on the walls, by opening up the shutters and letting in the fresh air, or by playing lots of lovely light music which swims around in the air. All these contribute towards creating a light environment in which to live. Of course your physical environment is important but even if you live with dark colours around you and your room rarely sees the light of day, you can still fill it up with your own positive energy which can lighten it up anyway. In this 3 cycle you may like to invite sunny people into your home environment who can fill it with positive energy.

When you are feeling positive during this 3 cycle you may find that relationships with people you live with become enhanced with this positivity too. Indeed if you have been very moody during your last Personal Year 2 then people may be relieved to see this optimistic attitude now sweeping through you. As a little of the 2 energy is still influencing you during this 3 cycle you may still get a little moody and emotional (a 2 quality) at times.

With this 3 energy you can find the sudden urge to party (yes, for the whole Personal Year cycle if you choose), particularly if you have a 3 in your chart already. Your home and your doors may be thrown open to all and sundry as your family, friends, workmates, children, animals and many of your acquaintances come around to party with you. This is because the 3 highlights social expression, and what better place to do it than at your home. However, sometimes you may also like to party alone with a good book in order to escape the (constant) deluge of people in your home.

During this 3 cycle you may find it difficult to keep your sense of humour, particularly when all your energy is going towards maintaining a happy but sometimes chaotic household. Perhaps the dog makes you laugh with the way it plays around and this brings a smile to your face, or your partner opens up a bottle of wine which spills all over his shirt or her dress. However, they may not find the latter funny, and you may be laughing on the other side of your face if they play a practical joke on you to test your abilities to keep laughing.

Laughter and play are some of the light qualities which this 3 energy brings into your home environment. Perhaps you become more playful in your words and self-expression, or the way you fool around physically with your mate. Indeed you may really enjoy the happy energies being brought into your home by being influenced by this number 3. Your home may be filled with laughter and giggles, and it's contagious in a positive way.

With the 3 influence you may find the need to develop your mind and spend hours alone reading up on interesting and fascinating subjects, or having deep intellectual conversation with others. Indeed you may get quite serious about your discussions (a quality of the 4 energy which influences the 3). However, with the influence of the 3 you may enjoy superficial chat and you may well find that this energy brings out your ability to make endless small talk. You may be a bit of a chatterbox and spend your time at home on the telephone eating away at your money with your relentless conversations about daily life, and even gossip!

The 3 energy means that you may be tempted to skim the surface with matters at home and try to avoid getting deep into conversation about important issues. Perhaps you talk your way around these issues by disappearing through the front door or by busying yourself with some activity around the home to avoid expressing yourself. In this 3 cycle you may even find that you are more bothered about how your home looks, materially and superficially, than the feelings or thoughts of those who live in it.

During this cycle there is an energy of expansion influencing you at home, and sometimes this out-flowing energy helps situations to be released and let go, and for you to simply let things flow. For example, if your partner wants to get married and you are avoiding expressing your feelings to him or her then eventually your relationship will expand one way or another anyway. The 3 energy always takes you further into life because every experience contributes towards your personal growth.

During this 3 Personal Year you may find yourself criticizing your home, the person or people you live with, and yourself at times. Perhaps with so much to do as a result of this action year you may be critical when things don't go right. Again, learning to be more laid back and relaxed can help you to focus on the important things in life, like bringing more love and laughter into your home.

PERSONAL YEAR
4

You are influenced by a 4 Personal Year and you may find that situations occur that influence the very foundations of your home life. Sometimes these situations can be easy to handle; you may work your way through them in a practical step-by-step way, but others may seem quite drastic. For example, if you are going through a divorce this may be one element which undermines the security of your home life. This may affect you physically as well, to the point where you become ill. During this 4 year there may be more stress at home in relation to practical issues.

With the influence of the 4, any physical changes within your home life are occurring this year in order to help to make your foundations more solid. You may not see this at the time because physical changes at home may mean disruption for a while, and you may feel unsettled within yourself and with the disharmony in your life. You may feel that you have a tremendous amount of inner conflict going on too (a quality of the 3, a little of which is influencing the 4). Perhaps you also find you are in conflict with people around you who are mirroring this inner process of change taking place within you.

However, your home life becomes solid and secure when you feel inner security, and when you have built strong inner foundations to weather all the different challenges and changes which come your way. Indeed, during this cycle, if you remain practical and down to earth, it can help you to get on with your life or to face situations occurring at home no matter what. For example, if you have a very sick family member to look after, by being practical about all the things you need to do, it can help to keep your foundations solid. This may help you to make the most out of each day and also help you to survive.

> Miranda has a sick child to whom she needs to give a tremendous amount of care and attention, but in this Personal Year 4 she feels she just can't cope any more. However, with the help of her husband she designs a new structure for their home life and, at the end of the day, this benefits everybody.

During a 4 Personal Year you may experience constant dramas at home, or rather you choose to make everything into a drama to brighten up a dull and boring home life. For example, even the tap leaking may be turned into an episode as you run around telling everyone about it. Even the plumber is subjected to hearing about what devastation it has created in your home. At times this year perhaps you also create very real dramas at home by not being down to earth and grounded. For example, by forgetting to remove a pan from the stove until it has burned your supper, or by leaving your back door unlocked when you are away on holiday for a week.

With the 4 energy, one of your biggest fears this year may be that you lose your home and your possessions. This may be because you feel that without these things you are nothing, or think that if you are without a home base you don't exist. However, it may help you to be realistic about your home situation this year, and also to remember that at the end of the day you still have (own) your own physical body which is actually your home.

Indeed, particularly if you have a 4 in your chart already, all kinds of issues may arise about your living accommodation during this Personal Year. You may find that you move into a new home, and although this may be exciting it can still be challenging for you at times, and perhaps it takes you some time to settle down. You may find you need to move out of your home suddenly due to a situation there, in which case you may not have your own home for a while. In a 4 year your home life is highlighted and as the 4 directly influences physical and material reality then this can influence where you live. However, during this cycle it may be helpful to be aware that wherever you live at the time can be your home even if you don't own it, be it a house, an apartment, a caravan, and so on.

The 4 energy is an earthy energy and you may find that you wish to pay a great deal of attention to your garden (or windowboxes if you don't have a garden). You may even like to bring plants, flowers and trees into your home to make it feel more earthy too. Perhaps you find that even if you don't normally have 'green fingers' then during this year your garden really blooms as the result of all the extra effort you put into it (from dusk until dawn). Perhaps you decide to build a herb garden at home to help improve your culinary skills. With this earthy 4 energy you may find that you pay much more attention to your food than you normally do, and perhaps you enjoy cooking more.

During this 4 Personal Year you may find that you wish to restructure your home by moving around objects or even bringing down walls in your home to change its physical appearance. Perhaps you even employ a professional feng shui consultant to help you find the best possible place for the arrangement of your home. Sometimes during this 4 cycle, by moving around objects in your home it may help 'stuck' areas to free up. In a 4 Personal Year you may be more concerned about the practical use of objects that can be of benefit to you, in order to make your life run more smoothly. Perhaps you go out and buy helpful gadgets this year. For example, tin openers that glide lids off cans, or liquidizers that are easy to clean, and so on.

You may spend more time doing DIY than paying attention to the people around you, and perhaps you find that you become preoccupied with your home. Even to the extent that you become irresponsible about work commitments (a 5 quality influencing this number 4). For example, perhaps you turn up late for work because you were just fixing a door handle or changing a lightbulb, and so on. However, within this 4 Year it may help you to place certain boundaries on yourself so that you know how long you can spend at work in order to make the most out of your home life, and vice versa. By doing this it can help you make the most out of relationships with people you live with too.

With the influence of the 4 you may find that the passion comes back into your home life. For example, if you had lost interest in your partner, or even in the home itself, then you may find a new surge of energy. Perhaps this passion means that you learn to enjoy life at home, maybe for the first time.

The 4 energy is challenging you to follow through on your family and home responsibilities. For example, you may start to wallpaper your home and then leave it half finished with the old and the new decoration openly displayed. This may cause great distress to those around you because it is unsettling. Or you may decide to buy a new home and although you have signed the agreements you forget to instruct your solicitor to transfer funds to the old owner, and your purchase falls through. Responsibility is a key issue this year in your home life and therefore areas where this is lacking may arise in order to teach you about this quality. So that you can learn through practical experience and move on.

During a 4 Personal Year, experiences at home can all contribute towards your grounding process and can help to keep you down to earth. Any upheavals at home are all there to challenge your ability to survive, and these changes may eventually help you to feel more secure about life from having 'been through the mill' at times.

PERSONAL YEAR
5

You have come through a 1 year of new opportunities at home, a 2 year of learning to bring balance into your home, a 3 year for expansion and a 4 year for laying foundations at home, and now in this 5 year you are working with the energy of change. Changes occur naturally and all the time but during this year you may be more ready to let go and to work with the changes to your home life. For example, if you have been going through a divorce in your last Personal Year 4 then you may well feel the need to move or even to push forward with it in order to move the situation on and into a new phase.

Sometimes during this 5 cycle you may find it challenging to adapt to constant changes in your home life, no matter how simple or complicated they are. For example, changing your regular eating times or the kind of food you eat may mean that you do not feel settled and enjoy your food as much as normal. Or you may find (particularly if you felt bogged down during your 4 cycle) that the change of eating habits inspires some new life and energy into your home life. Indeed if you change flatmates, lover or partner during this cycle then you may enjoy the stimulation from this too.

With the influence of the 5 you may feel very restless at home. Perhaps you move from one room to another talking to different people or doing different things, and perhaps you like this variety. Indeed you may enjoy the idea of spontaneity in whatever you do at home. You may feel so restless that there seems to be little satisfaction in anything. Perhaps you even feel like running away from your home *situation* at times. However, you can't run away from *you* (there's no escape) and it may help during this 5 cycle to face uncomfortable situations within yourself so that you can move on with your life. For example, if you feel that you are simply unable to communicate with your husband or wife, then running away may mean that you repeat the same pattern with your next partner all over again. Perhaps by admitting to yourself that you are fearful of communicating it may help you, particularly if you love your partner, to open up by expressing a few words, which may help him or her to do the same.

Communication is a quality that is highlighted during this 5 cycle and, particularly if you have this number in your chart already, you may find that issues at home arise as a result. For example, you have an argument with your flatmate because you asked him to buy some milk whilst he was shopping and he forgets. He says he doesn't remember you asking him to buy some. Indeed, you may think you are a good communicator but you may not be quite as clear as you think.

During this 5 cycle your external environment will mirror back to you exactly what your thoughts and words are. So if you find things running smoothly it may well be as a direct result of your clear communication, which helps everyone else around you too.

The number 5 highlights the possibility of unexpected events which pop up out of the blue in order to move your life forward. For example, perhaps you have a house guest who suddenly descends upon you and changes your whole home life around, or perhaps you have an accident at home (like tripping over the dog and injuring yourself) and you find this changes the home dynamic too. Within a 5 year, when there is a lot of energy moving about, it may help you to stay grounded (a little of this 4 quality is influencing the 5) by being practical during emergencies or during unexpected events. This can help everyone in your home environment.

The 5 energy influences adventures and fun and if life at home feels in a constant state of flux then you may enjoy throwing a party, or invite stimulating people around to your home to bring some light relief. For example, perhaps one of your friends has just returned from India and they bring wonderful photos or a video of the riches of this culture to show you. During a 5 cycle you may also find the urge to travel (with or without others who may live with you), and therefore your home life may be extended to wherever you live in the world at the time. For example, perhaps you travel to Thailand and you live in a monastery for months, and live by very simple means. Or you may travel up the Nile where a luxury cruise ship becomes your home for a while.

However, even though you may have a zest for fun this year and abandon your home for a while in order to live life out in the world at large you may also decide to travel into your mind at home. This is because the 5 influences mental activity and you may need to stimulate this too. For example, perhaps you spend your time at home 'surfing the Net', where you can read travel items, current affairs items, and with the influence of the 5 you may feel interested in most things on it. Perhaps you also enjoy getting more involved in information technology by learning about your computer.

The number 5 influences addictions and you may find that you become addicted to home life this year. This may mean that if you have been addicted to travelling the world, you may for example, suddenly become addicted to entertaining at home instead. Perhaps with constant parties, or intellectual dinners and discussions, and so on. You may also become addicted to somebody who lives with you or addicted to having many different visitors to your home, to help keep you stimulated with fresh energy. Indeed the 5 is a highly magnetic number and you may really enjoy many of the liaisons which come your way. Perhaps you enjoy constant change to satisfy your quest for life.

Life can be frantic at home during a 5 Personal Year and one way to cope with all the changes and movement in your life is by applying structure (a 4 quality influencing this number 5). By keeping a solid structure you may find that even when life is exceedingly busy the base lines are still in place. This may mean, for example, that you know that you can still manage to cook the food you need, have a bath, have somewhere to sleep, and to survive, during these times. Sometimes by drawing up your own basic home routine it can help those around you to get through the things they need to do each day too.

Sometimes during a 5 Personal Year you may need to restrict activities out of your home, for example, working, shopping, socializing, travelling, and so on, in order to work with the changes occurring at home. Perhaps you are happy with this and enjoy the stimulation of movement in your home life. Paradoxically, you may also restrict time spent at home in order to run away from situations, particularly where communication, or coping with big changes may be needed.

The 5 influences the senses, and you may spend some time during this 5 year cycle enjoying sensory delights with someone you love at home. Indeed this may turn you on so much that at times you do little else! Perhaps you design your home environment to suit your lifestyle or design your work time around the time you spend at home. During this 5 year fun and pleasure at home may be one way of coping with other changes occurring within your life.

PERSONAL YEAR
6

During a 6 Personal Year you are working with the final cycle of physical experiences during this current 9 year cycle. This is because next year your 7 cycle brings together this last 6 years of experience and your 8 and 9 cycles are times for cutting the ties and preparing yourself for your new 9 Personal Year cycle ahead. The 6 highlights wholeness and during this Personal Year there is the potential to find this to some degree at home, as a result of the many experiences you have been through during this last 5 years. Indeed during your whole life too.

Wholeness may mean that you are learning to take into consideration your whole family or group's needs or of those who live with you. For example, perhaps you would like to visit some friends but your partner really needs your loving care and attention at home. Sometimes by taking into consideration others' needs you get your own needs met too. So in this instance, if you choose to visit your friends it may be that your partner can benefit more from spending time alone at home than from having you around. By visiting your friends you may even return to your home in a more compassionate or caring mood than when you left.

Even if you live alone then you will generally have neighbours who are also part of your home community even though they don't live with you. Their energy influences your home, and indeed your whole community can too. For example, if you live in a neighbourhood which is very quiet and sedate then your home can benefit from this energy too. If you live near a busy main road then this fast-moving energy may mean there is a restless energy influencing your home, and so on. Sometimes when you are looking for an ideal home it may be helpful to take a good view of the whole neighbourhood to see how these energies may influence you, and what you want. During this 6 Personal Year you may be more sensitive to the energies of those around you at home and in your neighbourhood.

The number 6 influences collective needs and by paying attention to the needs of those around you in your home environment, it can help you to feel happier at home too. For example, you may wish to bring fresh lavender into the living-room, but if everyone else wants roses instead then you may be more than happy to comply. Of course, sometimes it may be that you feel you know what's best and you may go on and on about how wonderful your home would be with the smell of lavender in it. Your partner, family or whoever you live with may become so tired of your moaning about how much you want this beautiful smell in your home that they give in to your desires. With the influence of the 6 it is helpful for you to be aware of group responsibilities during this cycle and it may be that lavender is just what everybody needs! Particularly if having come out of your last 5 Personal Year cycle, there have been a lot of changes to work through at home for you and everybody.

With this group awareness influencing you you may also be aware of what you are not doing to maintain a sense of community at home. For example, playing your music loud may mean that you spoil the peace for others who live with you. Perhaps you are extra self-indulgent and turn your music up even louder when you receive complaints. You may at times become even more selfish during this year.

In this 6 cycle you are learning that your home is a collective environment, which means that any decisions needed are taken by the whole group, and not just by you.

This means that, for example, you all may decide which new sofa to buy, which rugs go where, and so on. If you live alone you may find your friends or family give their opinions about your final choice of furnishing too. Or you may choose things for your home which are collectively fashionable at the time, for example, the latest trends in design and so on.

With the influence of 6 energy you may find that you are more bothered about what your home looks like this year than the people in it. This is because the 6 highlights glamour, which means looking gorgeous and lovely, and all the tinsel that goes with it. You may spend more time and attention on decoration and tidying up, and when visitors come around you may be happier if they say they like the teacup than the tea inside it. However, during a 6 Personal Year you may also find that having a home that looks nice can help you to feel good in yourself. There is always a positive side to nature if you take a look behind the blinds and go deeper inside.

This year your animal instincts may be heightened. You may become more sensitive to the needs of those around you. Perhaps your instincts tell you that your visitor is not comfortable sitting in a certain chair or in certain company and therefore you take some swift action to change the situation. Possibly you use your psychic instincts to inform you when you have forgotten to do something like turning the central heating off at night so you don't roast alive.

You may feel a need for more emotional security in your life. Perhaps you are unsure about your own feelings towards a person or those you live with. Talking things through and expressing your emotions with those close to you may help in your home situation too. It may also help for you to learn to listen to those influencing your home situation. Sometimes, during this 6 cycle, you may need to make some decisions to help you feel more emotionally secure within your home environment. When you are doing this you may be swayed by your gut instincts, and also by what you feel is best for all the people concerned at home.

However, if you are displaying the qualities of selfishness and vindictiveness, then your instincts for survival may mean that you emotionally wound others to satisfy your own needs. At these times it may help to learn to be compassionate (a 6 quality) with yourself and to realize that you are trying to hurt other people because you feel so hurt inside yourself. The 6 energy means that you may be extremely sensitive to your home environment. By bringing in the 5 energy (a little of which influences this number 6) it can help you to use your positive thoughts, your logic and your mind to help get you through.

You may find that you are very loving and affectionate, and you may really enjoy nurturing and taking care of people at home. This can mean everything from making cups of coffee for your visitors to cooking a sumptuous meal for your lover, or giving him or her a wonderful massage too. You may really feel the need to provide a loving and nourishing home environment for everyone who comes in through your door. Indeed you may relish comfort this year and spend much of your income making your home a relaxing and inviting space, and spare no expense to make sure your guests are fed, watered, and surrounded by love.

Of course you love to be nurtured too and living in such a 'warm' space means that you can enjoy your own home comforts. During this 6 cycle you may buy a cat or dog who can also lavish love upon you, and vice versa, which all helps to create a homely environment for your visitors too. In this Personal Year 6 you may find that life revolves around your home more than during any other of your Personal Year cycle 1 to 9.

PERSONAL YEAR
7

You are influenced by the 7 energy during this cycle which completes your last 6 cycles of experiences and learning. You may therefore find that what efforts you have put into your home can be materialized during this Personal Year. For example, you may have been working on building a comfortable home where you can relax and feel safe, and during this cycle you may feel as though you have achieved this. During the last 6 cycles if you have been too relaxed about your home life and neglecting those you live with, you may also find that your home life may crumble in some respect this year.

The 7 energy highlights the spiritual and the material aspects of life. Therefore during this 7 year cycle if you are working with the material aspects you may become over-preoccupied with what your home looks like, physical activities at home, or with earning money in order to make your home a richer place to live. (Money is associated with the number 8, a little of its energy is influencing this 7 cycle.)

However, if you are working with the more spiritual aspects then you may experience life at home in a completely different way. You may place importance on meditation and time spent alone where you can contemplate the meaning of life. You may also encourage those you live with to be aware of their inner selves and the richness of their spirituality too. Perhaps you find, particularly if you have a 7 in your chart already, that you become impractical about money issues during this cycle as you focus too much attention on your inner life. For example, perhaps you forget to pay the household bills or just think, 'someone will pay them for me'. Therefore during this cycle you need to learn to take responsibility for yourself and to be aware of the consequences of being too spiritual at times.

You may lean more towards the spiritual or the material aspects of home life, and during this cycle you may be centred between these two dynamics. Therefore you are aware of the significance of both aspects in your home life. For example, you may go around your home lighting candles and drifting off into meditation from time to time and also spend time earning a living in order to maintain your home.

During this cycle you can also get more in contact with your spirituality by connecting with those at home. For example, you may realize that whatever situations occur between you and your boy- or girlfriend you may still feel connected spiritually. Indeed during this cycle it may feel more painful during times of crisis at home to lose your spiritual connection with those close to you, than to lose an emotional, mental or physical connection to them. However, this is an illusion because even if you do feel this loss at times, the whole of humanity is always connected spiritually because you are a part of one global soul.

During a 7 Personal Year if you have not generally paid any attention to your spirituality before then you may find that situations in life occur in order for you to explore this side of life. For example, if you get sick, lose your job, go through a divorce, experience a death in the family, all these things can take you deeper inside. You may then spend a great deal of time at home looking inwardly and soul searching in order to get in contact with your spirituality. Likewise, if you can normally be quite a dreamy person then you may find that this 7 energy helps to ground you so that you can materialize a home, things and people in your home, and be able to get your home life together too.

During a 7 year you may find that you lose your grip on reality, perhaps from spending too much time looking inward, or from being taken in by your illusions about life. For example, the 7 emphasizes the imagination and you may be dreamy about your home; perhaps you think it is a palace, or perhaps you dreamily see your relationships with those at home as larger than life. At these times it may help you to bring in some of the more material energy contained within this number in order to bring you back to physical reality.

You may also find that your imagination becomes a valuable tool. For example, you may make up imaginative food dishes for brilliant dinner parties (and then when everyone asks you for the recipe you may forget the ingredients because they came out of your head). Or you may be more imaginative in the way you decorate your home, and so on. Your intuition may guide you with life at home through your dreams. Perhaps you receive guidance through a dream about how to resolve a situation with a family member or someone with whom you live.

The number 7 contains an emotional element within it and therefore you may become ultra-sensitive to life this year. Perhaps you become easily emotional and hyper-sensitive to the little things which happen at home. As an example, you may cry with joy when a butterfly pops in through the window to see you. Or your sensitivity may mean that you feel easily hurt. This may be for instance because your cousin who is currently living with you doesn't finish his food and you think, 'He didn't eat all the food I made for him so I must be a hopeless cook!' During this cycle it may again help you to get a grip on reality by looking at the whole situation (a 6 quality influencing the 7 cycle). By stepping out of your own sensitivity and by putting everyone in the picture you may see the real reason behind circumstances in your home life. So your cousin may have been simply running off for an appointment and had in fact been annoyed that he was not able to finish your lovely food!

With a 7 influencing you this year you may be constantly worrying and anxious about life at home. You may worry from dawn until dusk. Will the postman deliver my letter on time? Will there be enough milk for breakfast for everyone? Can I get to the shops and back in order to buy the ingredients I need to bake a cake for my lunchtime guests? And so on. Anxieties may come in thick and fast and you may discover that current anxieties you have, for example about your health, are exacerbated during this 7 year cycle. Sometimes worrying means that situations are intensified as you put so much negative energy into them. However, the 7 also highlights the essential quality of trust, and by trusting that your day can run exactly as it is meant to, then it can help you to let go of your anxieties. So if you run out of milk you can simply find a milk substitute or drink something else. You can also apply this to the relationships you have at home, where worrying less may mean that relations go smoother than you think.

> Peter is an architect who works freelance. In this Personal Year 7 he finds himself worrying constantly that he will be out of work and unable to provide for his two small children. As a result, his anxiety makes everyone feel tense around him. However, he realizes that his behaviour is upsetting his family and decides to stop worrying, which coincidentally helps his work to flow.

During this 7 Personal Year you are being challenged to learn to appreciate life the way it is, and to learn to live in the moment and to be patient with life. So, for example, perhaps you appreciate someone else cooking for you at home, what a gift! Or you appreciate having good health, a loving partner, children, a roof over your head, a beautiful garden, and so on. When you put more energy into appreciating your home life right now it can make room for more positive situations to come your way.

This number 7 highlights nature and this encompasses all the positive and challenging aspects of life which you may experience during this cycle.

PERSONAL YEAR
8

You have completed 7 years within this 9 year cycle. During this 8 cycle you are now being asked to re-evaluate your experiences at home to see what you have learned, in order to move forward with your life. For example, you may have moved into your home with your new lover, married, had two children, all during the first 6 years of this cycle. During the 7th year you may have ironed out a few major challenges in your relationship with your husband or wife. Perhaps this year you may decide that it's time to move to a larger home, to have a third child, and so on. Or you may decide that you need to make some positive changes to improve your life at home.

During an 8 Personal Year you may find that great changes may occur as a result of all the re-evaluating you do with your life. This is because the 8 energy highlights birth and rebirth. Birth may mean you find completely new ways of living your life at home. Rebirth means that you may go through complete changes within yourself which can influence everyone you live with. Rebirth may occur as the result of you reliving old situations which have happened to you during this last 7 cycles of experience, within this 8 year. Perhaps you even revisit situations which occurred to you during previous cycles, or in your childhood and perhaps even baby memories come flooding back to you. Some of these memories may inspire you as you remember parts of yourself which you may have left behind. Other memories may disturb you, but looking at them with a new perspective (from the age you are at right now) may help you to cut the ties with the past during this 8 Personal Year.

Going through a rebirth can give you a new perspective on your home life.

Sometimes, the changes you experience in an 8 Personal Year may be your karma for all the intentions and actions you have carried out in your previous cycles. For example, if during your Personal Year cycle you played dirty by not paying your builder who decorated your old house before you sold it and moved on then this year you may find somebody doesn't pay you. However, you may have repaid your karma in your last 7 years for that lesson you were learning. Or perhaps you have learned the truth (the 8 cycle contains a little of this 7 quality within it) already, which is to be honest with your dealings in life.

With karma dealing you a firm hand this year you may find that you have potent karmic interactions with those at home. For example, when your old aunt visits you for supper you may be surprised by her extreme attitude towards you, and perhaps you feel the same about her too. Of course it may be that you are both simply having a bad day but more than likely it is as a result of you teaching each other lessons from your past. Perhaps your aunt brings you a bunch of red roses (even though it's not your birthday) and this may be your karma too.

During this 8 year cycle you may find that situations turn around in your life at home. For example, if you have had little success with your noisy neighbours then during this cycle they may move or change their behaviour towards you. It may also be that they don't change but your attitude towards them changes which helps your life at home to be a more positive experience. Life at home may also be turned around, for example, by a long lost relative turning up out of the blue. Perhaps your past then literally comes back to visit you.

With an 8 energy influencing your life this year you may feel the burden of responsibilities at home particularly heavy or cumbersome at times. However, this is only the case when you do not want to stand up for yourself and accept your karma. You may, for example, have gone to great expense to build a water aspect (an element of the 7 quality influencing this 8 year) in the living-room. Now you have to live with it as you run to the lavatory every so often because of the constant trickling water stimulating your internal water system! You could even have to put up with constant complaints from all your visitors or those who live with you at home. You may be stubborn and refuse to take it down because you do not want to 'lose face'. In this case it may help you to take responsibility and admit 'I made a mistake' in order to learn from your lessons and move on, and to live a more peaceful (the 7 energy influencing the 8) life.

With the 8 influencing you you may find that when you do little things around the home you really want to be recognized for it. This is your ego at work here saying 'Aren't I brilliant!' Perhaps your sister tells you how amazing the soufflé you made for supper was, or your partner tells you that the new curtains you put up fit perfectly – what a good job! There is a little of the 7 energy influencing this 8 cycle and sometimes you may simply like to feel one of its qualities – appreciation. However, being told you are impressive around the home may mean that you continue with the good work.

During this 8 cycle this energy may influence you to take charge of your life and to assert yourself at home. This may be in a situation where your partner has been bossing you around and getting his or her own way once too often. Or in situations at home where you feel out of control.

Being assertive can help you because with the 8's influence you may tend to let things go and be passive at times this year too, particularly if you have this number in your chart already. Gentle assertion may help you to feel in control of situations at home. Sometimes you may need to assert yourself even when you don't feel like you can be bothered, because you know it can improve your home life.

With the 8's influence at home you may find you are extra controlling towards those you live with. For example, perhaps you control the central heating thermostat to suit you to the exact degree, or perhaps you lay down the law about what time everyone can have their baths in order to fit around your routine. Perhaps you even try to control what your visitors, and those you live with, eat so that they consume what you think is good for them. Sometimes you may rigidly control those around you in order to satisfy your needs, or feel controlled by your need to control too. Wishing to control simply stems from fear, and sometimes by being easy-going and letting life flow, then life at home can work itself out perfectly well on its own.

The 8 is influencing you this Personal Year, therefore you may feel dominated by wilful people at home. Perhaps you enjoy being dominated for a while, particularly if you are regularly the one laying down the rules. Or perhaps being dominated means that you think you don't need to take final responsibility for your actions because other people are telling you what to do. However, in this 8 cycle you are learning to stand on your own two feet and if your partner or those you live with are always in charge then you are unable to practise this. So asserting your personal will and saying 'no' when someone tries to dominate you at home may also be helpful to your personal development and growth, and help them too.

The 8 energy is very magnetic and you may find that you draw in lots of people to your home. Perhaps your home gets a reputation for hosting parties for the rich and famous, or interesting people. Indeed with charm being another aspect contained within the 8 energy then you may be one of the most popular guests there. Perhaps your home becomes a place of power, superficial power given to you by your yearnings for recognition and inner personal power from feeling comfortable within yourself.

In this 8 cycle of your Personal Year, karma, fate, and destiny preside over your life at home.

PERSONAL YEAR
9

Life is constantly transforming itself, no minute is ever the same as the last or the next, and each experience you have is unique to this moment now. However, during this 9 cycle you may be very aware of the larger cycles which govern your life and the transformation it brings. That is the ending of this 9 Personal Year cycle which is taking place in order to prepare you for your next major 9 year cycle ahead.

At the ending and beginning of this 9 cycle you may be able to take a step back from your life and to take a good hard look at what changes need to be made. Perhaps you like most of your life already and feel the need to only make minor adjustments at home. Like changing the curtains, changing which nights you spend in or out, changing your love-in times with your partner, and so on. Or perhaps you need to make changes on a grander scale; changing your home, your living environment, or even changing your relationships with those you live with too.

However, with this 9 energy you have a whole year to consciously use your mind to discriminate about your life at home. This 9 energy also highlights great sensitivity and you may use your gut feelings to help you decide which way to move forward too. Sometimes your gut feelings may be swaying you in the way your emotions want you to go. So, for example, your feelings may be geared positively towards you moving in with your boy- or girlfriend and setting up a home with him. But when you do, you may find that it doesn't quite work out the way you expected it to. Perhaps your feelings told you that it would be all fire and passion and that there would be no fights over the bathroom in the morning, the logical facts, but your feelings can sometimes be wrong. During this 9 year it may help you to use your discriminating mind before jumping into situations ahead of time. Even though you can learn something positive from every experience you have in your life.

With the 9 influencing you you may find that you jump to conclusions easily about people and perhaps think your opinions are conclusive because you are either right or wrong. For example, perhaps you find your painter and decorator talking on the telephone when he should be working on your home, and you immediately think he is unreliable. Or you may see your neighbour delivering post through your door and deem them to be 'caring' people.

Sometimes it may help you to again take a step back and use your discriminating mind to assess situations at home before making rash opinions. So in these instances perhaps your decorator was answering the telephone when it rang for you (it was an urgent call), or perhaps he was ringing out for more building supplies so that he could complete his work. He may be totally reliable even though your first opinion said otherwise. Perhaps your neighbour may well have been delivering a letter which had gone astray, but perhaps they were being nosy and poking their nose through the letter-box at the same time. Maybe they weren't being quite as selfless as you first observed. Life is a constant series of experiences with each one leading to the next, and by casting your mind's eye over them all you can learn far more than deciphering each one as you go along.

During this 9 cycle you may find that you are more fiery and high-spirited and also more emotional than you are normally. This fiery energy may bring out your passion to enjoy your life at home, and you may channel all this energy into your creative gifts. Perhaps you enjoy passionate sex, or put lots of dynamic energy into your cooking, into playing a musical instrument, into painting, or into laughing and generally having a good time. Indeed, after the potentially heavy year you may have experienced in your last 8 cycle, it may help you during this 9 Personal Year to relax, loosen up, and enjoy yourself at home.

The 9 energy contains sub-elements of all the numbers between 1 and 9 and therefore you may need to learn to be adaptable this year to all the situations that come your way at home. For example, perhaps your boy- or girlfriend moves in, your housemate moves out, your close friend is sick and stays with you for a while, and so on. Perhaps these situations mean that you have to be adaptable, for example, about where you sleep, what time you get up for work, what you eat and so on.

At the end of this 9 year cycle you may understand more about many of the lessons you have learned along the way, and in your next 9 year cycle you can refine these lessons. Perhaps, for example, you have been learning in your last 2 Personal Year to weigh up your partner's needs with your own needs, in order to share a home together. During this 9 cycle you may learn to discriminate about your joint needs as you have worked on this quality together before. In this 9 year cycle you are literally refining the lessons you have learned before.

With a 9 influencing your home life you may be liberal in your attitude to your lifestyle and to those who live with you. Perhaps you usually set the dinner for your evening meal (you conform to tradition), but during this cycle you may be more casual about your meals. Perhaps you eat a 'television dinner' while watching a good movie, or you may eat your breakfast while still in your night clothes, and so on. Indeed with this 9 energy you may slump around the house in casual dress no matter what important guests are coming to visit you. This may be because you have liberated yourself from your last 8 cycle where you may have felt the need to be in control of your life.

During this 9 cycle you may feel the urge to experiment at home. If you own a house, for example, you may experiment by inviting different types of people to live there, or by experimenting with dinner parties where many different types of people visit your home. Perhaps you experiment with colour schemes too. Indeed the 9 energy may bring out an urge for you to paint or decorate your home in bright and loud colours which give a flamboyant feel to the place. Or you may experiment by bringing in various types of furniture or soft furnishings so that you can have different rooms to sit, work or play in, which all have a different look and feel to them. It may be that you have intellectual friends who all sit in one room, or artistic and creative friends who enjoy other areas of your home. Indeed it may seem like you are a chameleon this year as you learn to adapt to the people in your home and the ever-changing situations you find yourself in.

However, the 9 energy means that you find yourself seeking approval from those who live in or visit your home. Perhaps, for example, you decorate your bedroom the way your lover likes it, or you may buy a certain design of furniture because all your friends have the same. You may be fearful of standing out from the crowd, paradoxically, and want to go with the flow, and fit in with whoever is around at the time.

This 9 can inspire new energy into your home and it may truly seem like spring with new buds popping up all around you. However, these new buds travel up through old soil which has been nurturing the ground for a long time.

Likewise, you may feel the need to create a nurturing space at home so that the relationships which grow in it, and the lifestyle you lead, can be of benefit for your next new 9 year cycle of growth ahead. Learn to relax and let go as life takes you into the next phase of your home life.

4

PERSONAL YEARS AND YOUR RELATIONSHIPS

With every relationship that you have you can see from your Personal Year Numbers exactly what kind of issues may occur during each specific year. All life moves in cycles and by understanding more about yourself from your own cycles you can then learn more about your relationships with others. For example, if you are going through a 3 cycle where you are being asked to express yourself by bringing this quality to your awareness you may then observe how you go about doing this with others.

Each cycle brings the potential to learn many different fascinating aspects about yourself which you may not have previously been aware of, and can bring out qualities which are already there. When you go through each cycle you can attract people to you who are also learning about those same numbers or qualities contained within them. Sometimes this mirroring process is strong, in which case you may push up and resist that relationship, or want to go into it fully. This may manifest with a lover, for example, in you wishing to be with that person all the time. You may fall in love with them because you see qualities within them which seem dreamlike or perfect. But you are actually falling in love with yourself because the qualities you see are simply hidden aspects within yourself. Which is why when you fall out of love it is because you have recognized their special attributes which then become integrated within you too.

Of course you may still need to learn more about these qualities but perhaps with somebody else, and you may carry on focusing on different aspects of your relationship with your lover. This is the same scenario with all your relationships. That is, the lessons are simple, when you have learned about the specific qualities you need to learn from one person then you move on richer in experience.

Your Personal Year cycles can help to guide you through each Personal Year of your life within all your relationships.

PERSONAL YEAR
1

In a 1 cycle you are opening up to new opportunities within your relationships. This may mean that you are seeking to make a fresh start, and with your lover for example, you may introduce new elements into your love life together. Perhaps you may also have been through a difficult time, for example, in a relationship with your partner, during much of your last 9 year cycles. During this cycle a breath of fresh air may blow in and turn your relationships around for the better. It may also be that when you choose to look at your current relationship from a different viewpoint you decide that it is time to move on and find new opportunities elsewhere.

This 1 cycle can be very refreshing and it may even feel like you have just woken up into a whole new dimension. For example, if you have been working with the same boss for many years you may suddenly see him or her in a different light. Perhaps you see them as more astute, more caring, more intelligent, or even more reckless and so on. What you see mirrored back from those around you is of course a mirror of qualities you may have freshly discovered within yourself, hence you discover them in others. Sometimes this has a positive effect and at other times seeing aspects of yourself mirrored back to you is challenging. You may find that people whom you have got along with nicely for a long time suddenly become like strangers to you because you don't recognize some of their qualities which may also be contained in your shadow side.

If you meet a new lover, or make new friends or work associates in a 1 Personal Year then it is possible that you may all feel the pioneering spirit of the 1 energy which takes you forward with your lives. Each new relationship you form during this 1 cycle is helping you along your path or direction in life and can teach you new things about yourself. If you make new friends this year you may decide to go travelling around the world together. If you get married during this 1 cycle then you are aligning with new beginnings which is a part of this cycle. Sometimes experiences during this cycle can be life-changing, like having a baby for example. The number 1 may be the start of a whole new and exciting chapter in your life.

You may find that in order to move on and form new relationships this year a destructive element pervades your current relationships at times. For example, you may deliberately get angry with a boyfriend you are trying to leave and create arguments instead of being direct (a quality of the 1) and expressing to him what you feel. The breaking-down process in any of your relationships is a natural part of the moving-on process, particularly during this 1 cycle. You may find it helpful to bring in compassion (a quality of the 2, a little of which is influencing this 1 cycle), to help you open your heart to this process of moving on.

During this 1 cycle you may find that the level at which you connect in your relationships changes. For example, the number 1 influences the mental aspect and the mind and you may find that you connect more deeply on this level to people this year. Perhaps you decide to play chequers or Scrabble together instead of going dancing with your friends (perhaps you do both), or you may decide to enrol on an educational course to stimulate your mind. Sometimes this works well and you either make new acquaintances, friends and work colleagues to pursue your new interests with, or you may find that your interests rub up against those who live, work or play with you.

During this 1 cycle perhaps the focus in your relationships changes from one level to another. For example, you may have a work colleague who you relate to emotionally and this year you may open up to him or her sexually. Perhaps you also find that a relationship with a lover takes on a new direction – it may phase out into a close emotional bond when you break up. It is also possible that your relationships with people deepen too. All levels of connecting with people are significant, but sometimes you may want to connect with them in different ways than you do. The 1 energy carries you forward in the best possible way for you to go with all your relationships.

During this 1 cycle you may find that, particularly if you have a 1 in your chart already, you may be craving to move forward with your life and this year you may find yourself kicking up a fuss with anybody who stands in your way. For example, you may think that your husband is holding you back from taking a school diploma and get angry and frustrated about it. Or perhaps you think a work colleague is holding you back from promotion because they are putting you down in your boss's eyes at every available opportunity. This 1 cycle is encouraging you to go for what you want in life but self-doubts create excuses in your mind: why you cannot move forward with your life, and these are mirrored out in those around you. So instead of kicking up your heels in disgust it may be more productive to examine your own inner fears of doing what you want to do with your life during this year.

Sometimes, during this 1 Personal Year cycle you may find that you feel defeat in a relationship. This may be because you think that somebody should win or lose.

Perhaps you have been trying to teach your partner to respect that you need quiet time alone occasionally. Possibly every time you try to close the door and be by yourself for a while your partner creates excuses why he or she needs your attention. Your partner may act like this because you have not been direct in asking for your needs to be met. Sometimes feeling defeat can drive you on to put more effort into your relationships. At the end of the day you can learn something positive from all the experiences you have with others.

Within a 1 Personal Year you may feel more inhibited with those around you, even where previously you have felt relaxed and at ease. Perhaps you withdraw into your shell and become isolated from spending too much time on your own. However, if you have been through many changes during your last 9 year cycles then during this cycle you may benefit greatly from spending time on your own. However, this 1 cycle is influenced a little by the 2 energy and one of its qualities, openness, can help you to work through these feelings of isolation and enable you to open up to your partner.

During this 1 Personal Year you may find yourself being a victim, perhaps put upon by other people. As an example, your friends always expect you to take them out in your car for evenings out together, and to run them around, and you comply. Or your partner always expects you to pay for all the meals you have whenever you are out together, even though you earn less money, and you still pay. Sometimes being a victim can teach you to think of others' needs before your own, but it is also making room for others to dump more and more on you. There comes a point, however, perhaps during this 1 Personal Year, when you say 'no more' and you may choose to take action or to speak up for yourself in order for you to move on in those relationships in a positive way. Sometimes this means releasing a friendship, a spouse or a lover, or you may even move jobs in order to help you to take back your power, and to move on so that you can progress with your life.

PERSONAL YEAR
2

In a 2 Personal Year you are working towards finding harmony in all your relationships in your life, particularly if during your last 1 cycle you experienced some of those relationships breaking down on one level or another. Sometimes it is the chemistry between two people which creates this harmony, and at other times it may be because you choose to go along with what people say in order not to 'rock the boat'. In order to find harmony you may also experience dis-harmony for a while in your relationships too. For example, you may find that you have lots of arguments with your friend when you are working through various issues. Eventually life sorts itself out, and you may experience rough to smooth patches along the way, but at each turn you create the space to reach even deeper levels of harmony within yourself and your relationships.

You may find, during this 2 Personal Year, the need for peace in your life and in your relationships. This may mean that in order to get peace you walk away from a relationship which is draining you, or which is affecting all the other areas of your life. For example, if your lover is constantly defensive, touchy and confrontational you may respond accordingly and this does not make for a peaceful life. However, as the external always mirrors the internal, then finding your own inner peace during this cycle may really help you in your relations with people too. That is not to say you go around smiling all the time and being all peaches and cream to people, but that you create the space to breathe in your life. Perhaps you take up meditation or yoga which can also help to calm your mind, body and spirit.

The number 2 is associated with the emotional level of your body and during this cycle it may help you to be able to express your feelings openly to friends, family or whoever is around. This can also help to keep you calm, particularly if you have been stressed about a problem for a while because it can help to release tension. Indeed even when you are facing conflicts within your relationship, keeping calm can help you to resolve them faster or make it easier to handle them at times.

Sometimes you can also wallow in your emotions during this 2 cycle and you may let your feelings take over your whole life, and perhaps your relationships suffer. For example, if you are crying a lot at work because you have just split up with your partner then people may be compassionate with you for a while but they may run out of patience. Perhaps this is because they want you to be happy or because they feel disturbed or upset themselves by you crying all the time. It may help you to snap out of your wallowing when your boss feels courageous enough to ask you to get on with your work and leave your emotions outside. Sometimes if you do find yourself happily getting off on your feelings during this cycle it may help you to be aware of what this is doing to those who love you.

A 2 highlights cooperation and you may find that you enjoy working things out with your friends, family and work associates this year. Perhaps you like the idea of sitting down and discussing with your brother exactly what you would like to do, for example, for your parents' 15th wedding anniversary. You may enjoy coordinating your diaries in order to organize a big party for them. Cooperation can mean that you move through things faster, as joint efforts towards a goal mean there is double the energy available.

This year you may find that your relationships become easier if you bring in this positive quality of cooperation. Of course sometimes you may need to cooperate and not want to, but you may see positive results. For example, you may set up a business with a best friend and she may want you to sign a joint agreement with her. You may not want to because you feel your friendship is based on trust. However, even though you are friends it is important for you to cooperate on a professional level too. By doing so it can help to bring this element into your relationship.

The 2 energy highlights giving and receiving and you may notice how this plays itself out in your relationships this year. For example, perhaps you suddenly notice that you are giving a lot of time and energy to your mother who is emotionally demanding. Or that you seem to spend a lot of time listening to your friends talk about their problems. Perhaps your partner is always listening to you talk about your own feelings all the time too. If you have a 2 in your chart already, then during this cycle you may find you give more easily than receiving, or vice versa. However, balance is the key here and this 2 energy can help you to do just that.

You may find that when you give something or some quality to one person you receive back from another, even though you may want a certain person to give to you. This is also a natural part of the balancing process. However, you actually give and receive with everyone even when it doesn't seem like this. For example, you give emotionally to your sister and you receive back from her on the spiritual, mental or emotional level, or vice versa. This is part of the exchange of energies which constantly happens whether you are aware of it or not.

During a 2 Personal Year you may find that you become dependent emotionally on those around you. Perhaps this is because you become more sensitive to your feelings with this energy influencing you. For example, perhaps you have a sick relative and you feel like you cannot handle your own feelings of pain, anger or despair. Or perhaps your feelings and emotions get very intense when you are facing major changes in your life, even if these are positive situations, like getting married or having a child, for example. However, you need to learn to take responsibility for your feelings, and this may mean that you spend time writing down what you feel, or by allowing yourself to feel them and then let them go (a 3 quality, a little of which is influencing this number). During this 2 year it may help you to use your mind (a 1 quality influencing the 2) to help to refocus your energies elsewhere. For example, when you are feeling very emotional you may choose to focus on reading a book, watching a film, doing a chore around the house, or something positive which may help you to cope with your feelings.

During this 2 Personal Year you may have a tendency to sulk when others don't pander to your emotional needs. So for example, if you want your boyfriend to cuddle you and listen to you discuss your feelings and he just wants to switch off and watch television then you may be very moody indeed. With this 2 cycle you are learning to be aware that there is always more than just one person within a relationship and to give when it is needed. Paradoxically you may be more aware of the needs of those around you. Perhaps you take extra care to make sure they feel happy and that their voice is heard and their needs are met too.

This 2 energy brings in the quality of love to this Personal Year so even if you are not seeking a soul mate then one may seek you out during this cycle. This may mean that you find that special person who becomes an important part of your life. A soul mate is someone you have a deep connection with and who you seem to know instantly as soon as you meet them. Indeed your soul mate may be your best friend, someone you can share all your secrets with, or a partner. Or it may be someone you meet through work, and perhaps you have great success because you both see 'eye to eye' about work projects. The 2 highlights sharing and this is a wonderful quality to be working with at any time in life, but particularly during this 2 Personal Year cycle.

PERSONAL YEAR
3

During this 3 Personal Year you are working towards bringing expansion into all your relationships. This means, for example, that you may choose to get married this year as an expansion of an intimate relationship. Or expand a friendship by planning more activities with him or her and meeting up more often, and so on. Expansion usually happens when you have built a platform in your relationships from which to expand from, and often expansion comes as a natural extension to your joint goals or commitments together. Indeed every day your relationships are moving forward and expanding in some way whether you are conscious of it or not, because life and circumstances change all the time.

In all your relationships you will find that before things can expand there will be a period of contraction. For example, you may have been dating a partner for four years and having set the date for the wedding you suddenly get 'cold feet'. Perhaps you may even postpone the wedding until a later date, as you contract and withdraw (or resist life). However, on your wedding day you may feel one hundred per cent certain of your commitment, because the time you spent contracting gave you the impetus to move forward and expand in a much more dynamic way. Of course you may find at times that your relationships expand in ways other than what your heart desires. Sometimes life gives you the experiences you need, which does not always match exactly what you want.

During this 3 Personal Year cycle you are being asked to move on within your relationships by letting go and allowing the expansion in. For example, perhaps you have been resisting a relationship and during this cycle you let yourself go by allowing it in, or perhaps you allow yourself to expand further and deeper into a current relationship. Expansion can therefore mean allowing yourself to surrender to the ongoing process of life by going with the flow. That is not to say that you simply stand by and let your relationships take you over, but that you make decisions (a 2 quality, a little of which is influencing this 3 cycle) which can help you to make the most out of this flow.

Resistance is a natural part of the moving-forward process and without any resistance you may find that many relationships may not happen at all. Indeed, if things were too easy and there were no challenges, imagine what your life would be like. For example, you might go through each and every day agreeing with your partner on every concern and topic of conversation.

Sometimes you may move forward during this 3 Personal Year as the result of decisions you have made in your last 2 cycle (decision-making is one of the qualities of the 2 which is still influencing this 3 cycle to some degree). For example, if you found yourself arguing a lot with your father last year then you may decide to take his comments with a pinch of salt, and lighten up when he says things which charge your emotions. So this year you may be able to handle this relationship not only in a more caring way but also in a nonchalant manner. Perhaps you decided, at the end of your last 2 cycle, to take a more positive attitude towards your father in general, which expands into your relationship during this 3 Personal Year.

During this 3 cycle you may find that you will do anything to avoid conflict in your life and if you have one person, perhaps a friend, with whom you are in (constant) conflict then you may walk away from them or avoid them at times. This may be because with the 3 energy influencing you you feel very sensitive indeed, and you may find that people's emotions affect you deeply. For example, perhaps your parents are going through a lot of changes in their relationship and both are asking you to take sides, or to comfort one or other of them. In this situation you may do all you can to reconcile them, and you may avoid speaking to them if you feel their pain too deeply. However, a little of the 2 quality, balance, is influencing this 3 cycle, and you may apply this to your emotions and to your life, so that you do not go out of balance every time you experience conflict. You may find that your self-expression becomes blocked as the result of outer (which mirror the inner) conflicts in your relationships. Perhaps you do feel hurt about, for example, your lover and brother always rubbing each other up the wrong way and sniping at each other. However, it may help you, and them, to express your feelings to each of them and let them know how you feel. Perhaps this may open them up to discussing what they really feel about each other too. Paradoxically you may also find during this 3 cycle that you enjoy conflicts and like to set people off against each other. However, these conflicts may come back to haunt you as you may be drawn into arguments and situations. Perhaps you are particularly obnoxious to people or try to back away. In this cycle it may help you to bring in some of the 4 energy (a little of which influences this 3 cycle) to encourage you to learn to take responsibility for yourself.

In this 3 year of expansion you may find that you feel confused about what you want from your relationships, and feel that they don't move forward as fast as you would like them to. Perhaps you feel confused about whether your friend wants to remain a friend or become your lover, and because you are holding back on expressing yourself you do not find out. As the year goes on you may be wondering why nothing's happened to expand it in the way that you want. By opening up to your inner feelings and emotions and by being honest with yourself, you may find it easier to express yourself in all your relationships. Then the other person in the equation feels able to open up and express themselves honestly to you too. If you find it difficult to communicate your feelings at first you may find during this 3 cycle that you blabber out words which don't make sense, but with time you may be the one being told to shut up! This year you can expand with every relationship by growing rich in experience from the personal growth you receive.

This 3 year you may want to stretch your wings and fly and it may be that this zest for freedom brings some energy and enthusiasm into your relationships. For example, if you are married but rarely socialize, then you may find that the party-going, fun-loving aspects contained within this number spring to life and you become more social and enthusiastic about meeting people. This positive energy may influence your husband or wife, your friends and work colleagues, and indeed everyone you meet as you sparkle with vitality. Perhaps you discover the playful aspects of the 3 energy this year and include them in your life too. This can also mean playing around with people, but more positively the joyous activity of playing a part on life's stage.

Your sense of humour may be required at times, particularly if you are expanding and needing to be adaptable to the changes within (many of) your relationships. Perhaps you get on the soapbox and entertain people with jokes to lighten their day, or your witty jokes may go down really well in the boardroom. Perhaps some of your jokes become satirical, and you poke fun at others too by displaying the more challenging aspects to this number 3.

Within a 3 Personal Year you may be inspired by all the relationships in your life that are helping you to be yourself and teaching you about all the different parts of you.

PERSONAL YEAR
4

You have worked through 3 cycles within your relationships – new beginnings, balance, expansion – and now you are working at consolidating and feeling comfortable in your relationships. This may mean, for example, that if you got married last year, the relationships may settle down during this 4 cycle, or perhaps that you feel more comfortable within yourself. Consolidating your relationships means that you make them more solid or that you have clarity (a 5 quality, a little of which is influencing this number) about what the relationships are about.

Sometimes when you try to consolidate a friendship during this cycle you may feel there is nothing much between you because both of you have changed so much as individuals, which has changed the relationship. Therefore by consolidating, you may feel the need to change the foundations of your friendship in some way. For example, if you are friends because a third person keeps bringing you together, and that person moves out of your social circle, then you may have nothing much in common. Perhaps you both resolve to meet each other only on special occasions, and so on. Of course changes within your relationships may be subtle and you may hardly notice them as you quickly adapt to changing circumstances.

Life is constantly changing, but during this 4 cycle you may find that each little upset or change in the relationship turns into a drama. And with the 3 energy influencing the 4 cycle to some degree, you may be inclined to turn a crisis into a drama. For example, your boy- or girlfriend forgets to telephone to wish you good luck with your driving test which you are worried about. You may be so angry and hurt that you ring him up at work and scream at him, so much so that you lose what little cool you have left at the test. You are rude to the instructor and even though you drive reasonably well he is having an 'off day' too (or that's what you think), and he fails you. Then you make a big drama out of that too. During this 4 cycle it may sometimes help you if you learn to ground yourself by taking a deep breath before getting lost in emotion. And by finding out the facts (a 5 quality influencing the number 4); perhaps your boyfriend didn't call you because he was locked in a meeting at work or unable to use the telephone.

Sometimes dramas within a relationship may test your ability to keep on with that friend, that lover, your boss and so on, and it may be that if others are creating dramas in your life this year, you can help to ground them. This is because the 4 energy means you may be extra down to earth this year, and you are the one who remains practical in a storm. For example, your lover is locked out of the car and can't find the keys. You are the one who rings the locksmith, or the manufacturer to order duplicates, or to organize taxis or alternative temporary transport.

However, the 4 cycle highlights responsibility and you may find that by taking responsibility for others in your life you are failing to notice and take responsibility for yourself at times. Sometimes by simply focusing on your own needs and taking responsibility it can allow other people to do the same, particularly if you have a 4 in your chart already.

You may feel in a rut in one or all of your relationships, which is of course a mirror of how you feel about your own life too. Sometimes life may seem to drag on and on, with your relationship falling into a monotonous routine. Of course you may enjoy the security of knowing that you are, for example, going to meet your friends three lunchtimes a week, and so on. However, at other times your relationships may seem to stagnate during this 4 cycle as they fall into a rigid routine. So, if you always insist on making love at certain times or days of the week, then it may help you to bring in a little of the 5 energy (which is influencing this 4 cycle) with its quality of spontaneity.

Being in a rut can also mean that you have been working through a certain issue for a very long time, with your friend for example, but you may not be aware that it is time to move on. Perhaps that issue was loyalty, and now you have built up solid loyalty between you, or perhaps you have not been able to achieve this but you have both learned what you need from each other about this quality. Even if you do find yourself in a rut in your relationships during this Personal Year, it is still part of the process of moving forward because eventually all relationships move on.

With a 4 influencing you you may find that you see your relationships in a different light. Perhaps you become more realistic about your relationship with a lover, for example, and see that although you thought he was very romantic and slushy he was just putting on the style. Indeed with the 4 influencing you this year you may naturally feel romantic, even if you normally reject this kind of behaviour. Perhaps romance is the key to bringing out your passion within an intimate relationship this year. During this 4 cycle you may find that you enjoy your friendships more when you understand the facts rather than the fiction, because it can help you to know exactly where you stand, where you are, and what you may need to do.

In this 4 Personal Year you may feel you need some excitement and passion in your relationship in order to make you feel special and wanted. For example, you may feel mundane (it's an 'off day') and therefore your friend making a fuss of you, telling you what wonderful clothes you're wearing, what lovely hair you've got, and so on, may mean that you take even more care of your appearance and feel good. Perhaps your lover arranges a sensual dinner for two which may brighten up your relationship and make you feel extra special too.

During this cycle you may feel that you are struggling with a relationship and that it seems to be taking all your energy for it or you simply to survive. For example, you are living with a partner who each day seems to make more and more demands on your time and attention by asking you to do things for him or her. Or perhaps there are constant stresses in the relationship, like money, for example, which appears to be highlighted during this Personal Year. This 4 energy is asking you to be practical towards your material needs, and by doing so it may help to resolve some of the stress within your relationship.

Instead of struggling it may help you to learn to bring in some of the 3 energy (a little influences this 4 cycle), to let things flow. Indeed sometimes when you just do the best you can each day and let go and let the rest flow, problems can work themselves out and just drift away. Working through challenges in your relationship in a step-by-step manner (a little at a time), may also help you to release the need to struggle with your daily life, as you approach things systematically.

During this 4 Personal Year you may find that you attract people to you who can teach you more about friendship, which is one of the most important aspects contained within the 4 cycle. Indeed you may have passion and excitement in a relationship with a lover but at the end of the day it may be friendship which is the key to its success this year. This is because with the 4 energy influencing you, you may enjoy feeling secure, and making long-term friendships during this 4 Personal Year cycle may therefore be on your agenda.

PERSONAL YEAR
5

With the influence of the 5 in this Personal Year you may feel the need to bring more fun and adventurous elements into your relationships. Particularly if you found that in your last Personal Year 4 cycle you got stuck in a rut in some respects. For example, in an intimate relationship with a lover you may want to experiment with erotic sex inside or outside your home, particularly if your sex life has gone a bit dead. With friends this may mean organizing more social events than usual. Perhaps normally you play bridge with one group of people and you organize a concert out with them, or a walking holiday with them, and so on. With this 5 energy so associated with changes in general, you may find yourself doing things or saying things to those around you which are unexpected. You may even be surprised by your actions and words during this 5 cycle too.

The 5 is a number associated with the mind and sometimes your mind is so stimulated during this 5 cycle that you may say things without thinking. Sometimes you may find yourself being very verbal during this cycle even if you are not normally very expressive. Perhaps you are very perceptive in what you say to those around you and even though words seem to fly out of your mouth at times, you may be kind-hearted with your intent. For example, perhaps you tell your best friend that the colour of her dress makes her look drained, but you say it in such a way that she takes no offence. You may also find during this 5 cycle that you say nice things to people, but you are really angry underneath, therefore they are not received favourably. Indeed the same words can be expressed by many different people but it is their intent or the energy behind them which creates the reaction.

During this 5 Personal Year you are being challenged to communicate with those around you. Perhaps you are very good at communicating, particularly if you have a 5 in your chart already, or perhaps you are good at communicating with some of the people in your life, and hopeless with others. During this 5 cycle you may find yourself placing too much emphasis on the words you use to communicate and find that your message gets lost. You can also find yourself getting lost in words or that you lose others with your long vocabulary or your struggle over what it is you wish to say. However, the 5 also highlights clarity of thoughts and mind. No matter how good you are at communicating, by being clear about the true message you wish to communicate, others are more inclined to hear you loud and clear. So even if you use very few words you are able to truly communicate with those around you.

Of course communication takes place all the time on many different levels, like touch, body language, eye contact, telepathy, and so on. Words can be confusing, and sometimes a simple gesture, like putting your arm around someone you love, can communicate much more than words ever can. At other times by simply being with someone who is in a lot of pain or emotional turmoil can communicate that you care for them deeply, whether you touch them or not. During this 5 Personal Year you may be aware of all the ways in which you communicate and your external environment will mirror back to you your intent.

During this 5 Personal Year you may find that you suddenly become very magnetic and perhaps your friends, work colleagues and family become more demanding upon your social time. You may find yourself frantically running around trying to fit in all your diary of engagements. Socializing and having fun can be a wonderful way for you to enjoy this year and you may find that your communication skills polish up from the social contact. The 5 energy potentially brings in a love for life and most people you meet and the events which you attend may seem fascinating to you. This may also be mirrored in your growth and understanding of people which can develop during this 5 cycle.

This yearning to experience life (and your relationships) at full pace at times during this 5 cycle may mean that you can tire yourself out. Applying some of the 4 quality of stability (a little of the 4 energy influences this 5 cycle) may help you to be practical about what events you choose to attend, or what people you choose to see this year.

> Samantha recently got promoted to Managing Director of a beauty company, and in doing so now travels around the world. In this Personal Year 5 she gets to meet many different people, something she loves doing. She also manages to maintain a close connection with her lover by communicating with him regularly on the telephone, and makes an extra effort to communicate with him at home.

The 5 energy means that life can be unpredictable this year and even when you have lots of social arrangements 'tied up' you may find that these suddenly need to be changed. For example, you had arranged to meet your cousins and family for lunch in the country but because your car is malfunctioning you are forced to cancel your visit. Perhaps you get very angry indeed and you may issue a torrent of abuse because life has stopped you in your tracks. Or perhaps you blame yourself (a little of this 6 quality is contained within this 5 cycle) for not servicing your car recently. Life is constantly changing and sometimes it takes you off in a different direction to the one you had anticipated originally, but it's usually for the best. Perhaps in this instance the payoff was that you spent this time with your boy- or girlfriend and enjoyed a sensual lunch followed by an afternoon of passion instead.

During this 5 cycle you may be only too aware of just how changeable life really is. Perhaps you feel stable in your relationship with a partner, for example, the next minute you're in the middle of a flaming argument, and later it is back to stability again. Perhaps this year you may suddenly break up with your partner, or suddenly decide to enjoy yourself flitting from one lover to the next (restlessness is also a aspect contained within this 5 energy). If you have also been challenged within a current relationship by your lack of commitment then this year may be the time you suddenly decide to go for commitment. During this 5 cycle, life keeps you on your toes so that you get to learn more about your relationships and so that you do not rest on your laurels but learn to put more energy into life.

Challenges may also occur during this 5 Personal Year as the result of your procrastination about what you want to do about certain relationships, and you may 'tear your hair out' trying to decide what to do. For example, do you want to go the the movies with your friends tonight, stay at home with your lover, go to the gym, or what? You may be a popular person and you may procrastinate because you feel you have too much choice of companionship. But you may also find that you miss out on life by your inability to make decisions, or by your changeable moods highlighted by this 5 energy.

Sometimes this 5 energy may mean that you want to form or develop relationships that can help you go more deeply into life. For example, a friend is experienced sexually and opens up a new perspective on your relationships and on life during this 5 cycle. Perhaps another friend teaches you how to develop your mind and this can help to enrich all your relationships, or helps to open you up to your intuition, and so on. Indeed, this year you may wish to educate yourself and life seems to be constantly teaching you things.

During this 5 Personal Year you may wish to see the logic in your relationships. For example, why you and your partner behave like you do towards each other, and so on. This is because the 5 influences the scientific mind and you may wish to view your relationships from every different angle in order to understand what they are about.

PERSONAL YEAR
6

During this cycle all your relationships are highlighted to teach you about wholeness within your life. In life everybody is a part of everyone else as we are all human. However, you attract different people to you to teach you different things. Piecing together all these different elements which you are learning from them and integrating within yourself can help you to find wholeness. Of course wholeness cannot be achieved as such, because wholeness would mean perfection on every level, mind, body and spirit, and nobody is perfect. Although everyone is perfect in their own way. You may have one friend who is teaching you about respect, a parent who is teaching you about responsibility, a work colleague who is showing you how to collaborate, and so on.

You may find, during this Personal Year 6 cycle, that you tend to keep attracting the same situations in your relationships, and this is in order for you to work on some of its qualities intensely. It's a bit like playing the same old tune on a piano until it is perfect (except you may end up with repetitive strain injury and you may also find with this 6 energy that you feel it's never perfect). For example, nurturing is one quality contained within the 6 potential. Perhaps your partner teaches you a lot about this by showing you how to prepare gorgeous food, or your lover teaches you how to do pilates (a form of stretch and breathing exercise) in order to help you keep fit, and so on. During this 6 cycle you may get carried away with these lessons, by over-exercising, over-cooking and eating, and nurturing yourself until you become self-indulgent.

Perhaps you find that you want to spend all your time with the people who are teaching you these things too.

You may also become preoccupied with your physical appearance and want to look good all the time during this cycle, but even when you do look great you may still feel that you don't look perfect. Indeed, even though your lover and everyone else tells you how wonderful you look you may not be satisfied.

Sometimes you may find yourself taken in by the appearance of others and feel hurt when they don't turn out to be the 'nice' people you thought they were. For example, if you are a woman, you might decide to go out with the chap from work who always dresses really well and looks gorgeous, and he is a real charmer too. On your date at the restaurant he sits opposite the glass mirror behind you and spends more time looking at his reflection, or in the bathroom, than he does looking at you. Of course looks count and are enormously important, but it doesn't make someone a nice person, the same way that just because a car is attractive doesn't mean the engine works well. During this 6 cycle it may help you to cast a glance underneath the surface to see what lies beneath all of those people you have relationships with. Glamour doesn't count for everything.

In addition to looking good this year you may also like to feel good too. This is because the 6 highlights the feel-good factor and the 6 is associated with your feelings. During this cycle you may therefore choose to spend your time with those you feel good with, or perhaps you can encourage them to feel good too. Feeling good about those you are in a relationship with really stems from feeling good yourself and this means loving yourself. Indeed life can throw every situation at you but because you feel good about yourself and life then you can handle them in a more positive way. However, perhaps you get annoyed when you get that little spot on your face, but giving it some loving kindness may even help it to go away! Or help you to accept that your skin can't look perfect very day.

> In this Personal Year 6, Marie decides to visit her dentist. (She has been putting it off for ages.) She chipped two front teeth in an accident and now she wants dental treatment in order to improve her physical appearance. As a result, she feels really good about herself and more loveable. The treatment also improves her health generally.

The 6 energy highlights your emotional sensitivity and it may be that you enjoy connecting with those close to you on this level during this year. For example, you may find that you are able to open up to your lover more easily and therefore have a more intimate relationship because of this. Or perhaps your boss opens up and tells you why she has been so temperamental recently and this may enable you to connect on this level too. However, particularly if you have a 6 in your chart already, then you may also find this year is too painful for you emotionally as it heightens your sensitivity. On the other hand this year can help you to get in contact with deep emotions which you never knew existed and which as they say are 'better out than in'.

Releasing emotions in a constructive way, that is by being clear (a 5 quality a little of which is contained within the 6) about your feelings, and then letting them go, can help you in your relationships during this 6 cycle.

During this 6 Personal Year you may find yourself putting duty before your own needs. For example, perhaps you had arranged to go for a manicure and to the hairdressers but your husband needs you to take your children to see his mother who is sick. With this 6 influence you may find yourself completely surrendering to what is needed at times rather than following your own personal needs and desires. However, you may also expect your family, friends and work colleagues to serve you, and you may want them to drop everything in order to do their duty for you as well.

You may find that you are more aware of your group's needs during this 6 cycle, and perhaps you find yourself taking on more responsibilities for them too. For example, you may feel the need to provide work for them, money for them, love and food for them, and so on, and you may even feel the protective instinct too. In this Personal Year your ability to tune into your instincts (or your gut feelings) is highlighted, therefore you may be guided by these too.

However, sometimes you may think your feelings are telling you what actions to use or words to say, but your own personal desires may get in the way. For example, perhaps you feel that your partner should buy green clothes because your instinct is telling you that's what he or she needs. However, they may loathe green but because they love you they agree to give green a trial basis. But they come home from work that evening in a bad mood as they have felt uncomfortable all day. Green is one colour which is associated with the number 6 and you may have been projecting on to them your gut feelings about what it was that *you* actually needed during this 6 cycle. In this 6 year it may help you to incorporate the 5 quality of logic (a little of this 5 energy influences the 6) so that you can use your head and your heart when making decisions about your relationships.

You may find that at times you glaze over the truth about your relationships this year by wearing pink-coloured spectacles, and by refusing to look at what is going on underneath. Even though you may be only too aware of the consequences. As a result, you may find that situations get out of hand. For example, you think your partner is having an affair with somebody, but by avoiding expressing your feelings or talking about this to them directly the situation deepens. Until one day they tell you. Perhaps you thought they were so nice that they wouldn't do something like that to you, and don't accept any part you may have played in creating the situation. However, all relationships can teach you more about yourself and even when some lessons seem painful there is still plenty for you to learn, so that you don't repeat these same patterns again. With a little of the 5 energy influencing this 6 cycle, working with facts may help you to make the most out of all your relationships.

With the 6 energy influencing you this Personal Year you may like to become a master of pleasure; but painful situations can also teach you to make the most out of the good times which come your way in all your relationships this year.

PERSONAL YEAR
7

You are working towards pulling together the experiences you have gone through within your last 6 year cycles during this 7 Personal Year. Therefore relationships may bloom and blossom because you have been putting in time and energy to help them do so, or you may feel a sense of loss if they don't go the way you planned. For example, one of the qualities highlighted this year is trust, and this is an essential component in any relationship.

However, what this may actually signify is that you fail to trust yourself, and therefore you may not trust others. For example, in an intimate relationship with your partner you may project that he or she may be wanting to go off and have affairs with others in the vicinity. But it may actually be you who does not trust yourself not to go off with other lovers, and you project on to your partner by thinking he or she is untrustworthy. Of course there may well be other reasons to think this is so too. During this 7 year you may also be a master of illusion as you pull the wool over (say) your lover's eyes by saying 'trust me' as you sneak off and do something which denies that trust. Within this 7 cycle you may therefore find that your trust is broken with people around you. This year you can both learn to trust the process of life.

Relationships mirror back to you qualities and issues which you need to work with and therefore by taking a look inside yourself during this 7 cycle it may help you to find your inner truth. Sometimes by realizing the truth about a situation in a relationship it also helps others to do the same, and this will be so particularly if you have a 7 in your chart already. However, truth is really about seeing life as it is, not as you would like it to be, however challenging that may be. For example, have you ever been in a relationship with a partner and thought, 'I want it to be like this, or like that'? You want to be anywhere but where you are right then. For instance with another partner, doing something else, in another country, and so on. All these 'ifs' are part of the dreamy illusion of the 7 energy catching up with you, and at the end of the day you can only live in the moment. Ponder on that.

The 7 energy highlights introspection and a need to connect with your spirituality. Perhaps this enables you to feel a stronger spiritual connection to those around you. Sometimes you may be too dreamy during this 7 cycle as you drift off into the world of your imagination where nobody can find you or reach you except those on the same wavelength. For this reason you may sit meditating with friends for hours or find that you isolate yourself so much from the outside world that at times you find it difficult to string two words together. Spirituality is actually a natural state of connection which exists between all people. However, sometimes looking inward can help you to *feel* this spiritual connection with others, but it is always there whether you are aware of it or not. If you often feel disconnected from people then it may help you, during this 7 Personal Year, to feel this spiritual connection with those close to you.

During a 7 cycle you may be dreamy but sometimes this imagination can help guide you to exactly what you want in your life. For example, you may dream of a strong, dark, handsome man who turns you on, or a woman who is motherly and nurturing who likes to protect you. However, the 7 energy can also help you to be incredibly productive, particularly when you are focusing your mind positively on what it is you want, and you may materialize your dream person straight into your life. Of course that is not to say that you are happy about him or her once you've done so (with a little of the 6 energy influencing this 7 cycle then you may be looking for perfection). Perhaps you have arranged to meet a close friend at the train station to go to an event out of town. However, you do not really want to go with your friend, you want to spend time by yourself. On the way there you are thinking intently 'I don't want to go', and although you wait where you were due to meet your friend, he or she doesn't turn up much to your relief as you board the train by yourself. Therefore it may be helpful for you to be acutely aware of your thoughts during this 7 cycle because they help to create your reality.

During this 7 Personal Year you may be blunt in your speech or sharp or harsh with people at times, and sometimes you may be like this because you do not realize what it is that you are saying because you are off dreaming. You may not intend to deliberately hurt people, although you still need to take responsibility for your words and your actions. For example, your mind is elsewhere when you are talking with your father, and when he asks you a question, you snap at him with the response, or come out with some blunt truth. He may feel that you are jolly uncaring and so may others around you during this 7 cycle. People may even feel that you are very rude or even nasty at times too.

However, you may react like this because you are so self-centred and cannot see the whole picture (a 6 quality, a little of which influences this 7 cycle). Perhaps you are insensitive to their feelings or to their needs as nobody else seems to exist. It may help you during this Personal Year to be realistic and to put yourself in other people's shoes at times, particularly if you wish to remain on friendly terms with some of the people in your life.

In a 7 Personal Year you may find that you become hypersensitive to other people's remarks too and you may withdraw into your shell if you feel unable to cope with your feelings. For example, if your boyfriend mentions something about your figure being slightly overweight then you may withdraw from sight. Sometimes when people say things which hurt you it may be because you feel there is some truth in their remarks.

However, during this 7 year you are likely to go off at a tangent and exaggerate remarks with your wonderful imagination. So your boyfriend saying 'Your skirt looks tight' may translate into 'I'm overweight' in your own eyes. During this cycle you are particularly being asked to 'get real' about your relationships and to stop taking things personally. In this instance, perhaps your boyfriend feels rather overweight himself and is very sensitive about this, and so he sees it mirrored in you and others around him.

In a 7 Personal Year you may find your emotions are sometimes destructive in your relationships. You may feel on an emotional seesaw that seems to go up and down as a result of your heightened sensitivity. For example, if you are always moody and snappy then your live-in lover may not put up with you. However, if this is a problem for others it may be because your emotions are opening them up to their emotions too which they may not care to do. Indeed people may react strongly to you, and you may be a catalyst in their personal development process.

During a 7 Personal Year you may find you would like to take a rest from certain relationships, particularly if you have been in them for a long time. For example, you see your work colleagues at work and then socialize with them in the evenings too. Sometimes resting for a while can help you to analyse relationships so that you can return to them at a later day (perhaps in this 7 cycle) with renewed energy and vitality. You may also find that taking a rest from those around you even for 5 minutes can help you during this year.

PERSONAL YEAR 8

This is your 8 Personal Year and whatever experiences you
have materialized during the last 7 Personal Year cycles can
now work themselves out through this 8 energy of karma.
Karma is often blatantly visible within all your relationships but this year, even if you have not been aware of this
quality before, it may be particularly evident in your life.
Karma is indeed the law of cause and effect, but the lessons
associated with it are simple. However, it may take you
some time to learn them (even a lifetime or many lifetimes) and therefore they may become major issues at
times. For example, perhaps you can generally be quite
irresponsible. Perhaps you are irresponsible towards a
friend by not buying their train ticket when they asked you
to help them out, and he or she is late departing as a result.
This may have been because you were too busy reading
magazines in the station shop and you simply forgot. In this
cycle you may find that someone (your friend or someone
else) causes you a challenge by being irresponsible towards
you too.

However, when you learn the lessons that karma is
teaching you fully, then you can move on. For example, you
may have been irresponsible for many, many years and this
one lesson with your friend may have improved your ability
to take responsibility for yourself. Of course you can be
blessed by the karma of reward during this cycle and you
may get back some of the positive energy you have put out
into your relationships too.

During this 8 cycle you may find that you cut the ties
with certain people in your life. This means that you may

sever the link with those who no longer seem to be serving you with your lessons in life, and vice versa. Perhaps you have learned all you needed to from them in the last 7 Personal Years or even previous to that. You may feel stronger as a result as you feel complete with these people in some way. You may also feel emotional, vulnerable and sensitive (7 qualities, a little of which is influencing this 8 cycle) about this too.

Cutting the ties during this cycle may, however, not mean the end to a relationship. It may actually be able to continue on another level, and it can even help to deepen your relationship together too. For example, you have been through happy times, and also a lot of trauma as the result of illness during this last 7 years with your partner. But you may find that cutting the ties with this part of your life by consciously letting go of your attachment to your partner or what has happened between you both, may help your relationship to regenerate in a positive way. Of course fate plays a hand here too, and you may be playing out karma from your past (lives), and no matter what you do the relationship will take the course it is meant to.

During this 8 cycle you may find that when you meet new people in your life, be it a potential friend, lover, work mate or family relation, you may find that you instantly bond with them. It may feel like you have met them before, for example, or that you just *know* them as soon as you meet. Perhaps memories of past situations (even past lives) come flooding back to you too. For example, you meet a stranger on an aeroplane and find that you don't stop talking for the whole journey and you exchange telephone numbers at the end of the flight. Within a week you may have struck up a business deal with that person, dated them, or socialized with them many times, as you expand upon the deep connection you have made. Of course this is not the same as whirlwind connections you may make with acquaintances because you both have things in common. But all relationships can teach you something.

In all your relationships you can tell those with whom you have strong karmic ties because these are the people who seem to make a big impact upon your life. You may sometimes find that you can never seem to get away from people with whom you have these ties, and they may keep popping up everywhere you turn in your life. Or you may not see them often but each time you do they make a big impression upon you, and vice versa. These connections are drawing you in because you need to connect on some levels. Karmic relationships are very powerful and they can sometimes instigate great changes in your life. They can also help you to grow as a person because the lessons they teach are often very potent indeed.

All karma that works itself out within your relationships is actually teaching you about responsibility, which is another aspect of the 8 energy highlighted during this Personal Year. However, everyone needs lessons to learn and if everyone was perfectly responsible one hundred per cent of the time there may be no need for you to repay karma. It may also be helpful for you to be aware that karma from the collective consciousness and planetary karma greatly influences your relationships too and particularly during this 8 cycle.

During this 8 Personal Year you may be re-evaluating your life, and you may therefore find that ex-lovers, partners, relatives or work colleagues reappear in your life. Perhaps this is to fulfil some past karma together. Sometimes rekindling the past can be a wonderful experience as you remember all the wonderful times you have spent together. At other times, meeting with people from your past may help you to clear up unresolved matters between you both by re-evaluating what has happened.

In this 8 Personal Year cycle you may feel more assertive. Perhaps this changes the dynamic with some of your relationships, like with a girlfriend or boyfriend, for example, by you suddenly standing up for yourself. Sometimes this may feel threatening to those around you, particularly if they are not used to you applying this quality to these relationships. Indeed, the 8 also highlights the quality of control, and if your partner is used to you doing as he or she says then your self-assertion, and taking back your self-control, may not be welcome. Sometimes you may find that you become very controlling this year too. Perhaps you try to control your wife or husband because you feel they may leave you, or try to control your friend so that he or she does what you think is best for them and you, and so on. However, situations in this 8 Personal Year may also mean that you feel out of control at times, which may be one of life's little lessons to teach you to simply let life flow.

You may find that you are really able to 'find your feet' within a relationship during this 8 year cycle and you may also find that it goes from strength to strength. For example, your relationship with your lover may have been working itself out nicely for the past 3 years but during this 8 cycle the whole relationship may feel stronger because you have learned to find your own personal power and inner strength. Therefore you may feel more at ease within your relationships, which may also empower others to be the same.

During this 8 cycle you may take your relationships very seriously indeed and it may help you to bring in a little of the 9 quality, that is to be liberal with yourself, in order for you to lighten up and let go into life. Indeed you may be rather bossy, domineering and bullish with people during this cycle. And if you don't lighten up then your ego may well take a splattering if your friends, for example, decide to tell you the truth (a 7 quality which influences this 8 cycle to some degree) about your behaviour which can be heavy at times. Perhaps you may even become possessive during this cycle or experience this yourself within a relationship, which is again a calling for you to relax and let things flow. You may try to intellectualize what to do regarding your relationships this year too as the use of your mind may be strong during this cycle.

PERSONAL YEAR
9

You are now in the ending of a 9 year cycle and you are preparing for your next 9 year cycle in your relationships. Therefore you may find that some relationships come to a natural conclusion during this cycle. Or that other relationships have naturally rearranged themselves into a form that can take you both together into your next 9 year cycle. Of course relationships begin and end, form and reform, on a daily basis too, but you can be more aware of this larger cycle playing itself out this year. This 9 cycle is therefore highlighting a time for transformation in all your relationships.

During this Personal Year you may find that you feel the need to take the lead in a relationship. Perhaps this is because, for example, you have been led along the path by a partner for a long time and now it is time for you to take the reins. Particularly if you have a 9 in your chart already you may thrive off this leadership role. At other times you may be required to take the lead as a result of circumstances beyond your control. For example, your partner is sick and cannot look after the children for a while so you need to lead them through this situation. Of course, sometimes when it appears that one person is leading in a relationship you may be aware that the other person is subtly directing it in some way. For example, you are out at dinner with your new lover and you suggest, 'The fish is excellent, what do you think?', but you make it seem as though your lover has made the decision about what you both should eat as he or she orders the food for you.

During this 9 cycle you may find that you become very selective about your friends, where you go, what you do, who you see and when, and so on. This may be because you feel superior to them (as the result of a little of the 1 energy influencing this 9 cycle), or because you like to only associate with – in your eyes – the best people around. Perhaps you behave like this as the result of a perfectionist quality, an aspect of the 9 energy which is influencing you this year. You may even put the people you normally associate with (and permit into your life) on a pedestal by separating them out from everyone else. However, when you become 'exclusive' with your taste within your relationships, then you are also excluding life and pushing away people and situations which may help you to grow rich from those experiences. Of course that is not to say that you allow everyone who wants to come in through your doors, but to be more open to people and towards life.

Sometimes, during this 9 cycle, you may be – paradoxically – very liberal and be very accepting and understanding of people. Perhaps you attract all kinds of people from all walks of life as they feel safe and comfortable to talk or to be with you. Indeed you may be very compassionate this year with the 9 energy influencing you, and friends, strangers and loved ones may come to you with their problems knowing that you will have a big open heart and be full of compassion for them. You may be extra loving, caring and warm towards those you meet this year, which is also an added bonus in an intimate relationship as it opens the doors for intimacy and closeness on other levels.

In this 9 Personal Year you may find that you are truly inspired by the people around you. Perhaps your relationship with your boss which is so open and honest inspires you, or your relationship with your lover inspires you simply to be yourself. This 9 energy has a creative feel to it and therefore you may find that a painting which your partner gives you, a meal which your father makes for you, or a love letter inspires you too. Perhaps you are inspiring them to do these wonderful things for you. Allowing yourself to be inspired by even the tiniest things or by the people in your life can be a wonderful way for you to experience this 9 cycle, particularly during challenging times within your relationships.

This year you may find that you need to have faith that challenges in a relationship can work themselves out in the best possible way. For example, you may be in a relationship with a partner who is mentally abusive (an 8 quality, a little of which is influencing this number). Perhaps you find yourself being too laid back and simply accepting his or her behaviour as okay, which may encourage them to carry on the same. Perhaps during your last 8 Personal Year cycle you did try to do something about it by being aggressive back but that compounded the problem, and in this current cycle you may have lost faith that things can ever change.

However, life is constantly changing and moves you on regardless, and this is particularly evident during the transformation period during this 9 year cycle, although sometimes you need to help life to move along. Indeed you may have faith that life can work out better with someone else and let go of these tired patterns you have both created in this relationship. Or you may resolve to change the situation between you – in which case you may transform to learn some lessons together into your next 9 year cycle too.

Sometimes, when you face big challenges in your relationships during this cycle you may turn towards your spirituality or to religion to help get you through. Perhaps you go to church, a temple or a monastery to pray, meditate, or chant, or you simply feel your deep connection to the whole of humanity. Going inside of yourself for inner connection and strength may help to free up your attitude to situations within your relationships. And allow the higher will which governs everyone on earth to work out what is best for you. The 9 energy being associated with the spiritual elements of life may mean that you find you are extra sensitive or even emotional as you learn to open up to things this year.

During this 9 Personal Year you may be full of high expectations from those you are in a relationship with, which may mean that you sometimes feel disappointed with the people around you. For example, perhaps your lovelife has lost its passion and you expect your lover to make it perfect for you. Or you may expect your sister to meet you for lunch when you want her to and are disappointed when she says that she can't fit you in that day, and so on. Sometimes expectation can be a positive element to bring into your life this year because it can teach you about things you want from your relationships and life. In which case you may already know, with the wisdom of this 9 energy influencing you, that you don't always get what you want in life but you certainly get what you need.

During this 9 cycle you may find that you want to make your own rules and regulations about what you expect and want from some of your relationships. Perhaps you like the idea that a relationship goes the right way or the way you want it to go so you try to make sure it does by laying down the rules. However, there are higher rules which govern everybody and you may find that even when you try your hardest your rules simply fade away. For example, you say 'I want you to be home at 6pm for dinner every weekday' but your partner's boss may make a new rule that he or she needs to work until 7pm every night, which overlooks your personal desires or needs.

This 9 energy highlights selflessness and sometimes taking into consideration your partner's needs may make for a more adaptable and potentially a more successful relationship. Perhaps you can actually allow yourself to enjoy dinner at 6pm, 8pm, or even midnight with your partner.

5

A SUMMARY OF
THE LESSONS 1–9

Having read this book you may now understand that numbers are intricate little energies which weave their way through a never-ending cycle in your life. From a zero, where all concepts begin, through to the cycles 1 to 9, and then on to a new 1 to 9 cycle, and so on. As you go through each cycle, you learn a little bit more about yourself from the experiences these number cycles impart.

By observing how these cycles play themselves out in your life you can start to get a feel about what each number is teaching you. For example, perhaps during the 2 cycle you are learning to relate to people, and so on. The lessons associated with each number are very simple, but it is the situations you create in order to learn about those lessons that are of relevance to you, and these may seem complicated at the time.

However, life works itself out in its own way and you may eventually be able to see the positive side to all the lessons you are learning, or have learned in life. Numerology can help you do this by casting some light upon these situations, so that they highlight the strengths, challenges and the potential from each cycle. Whether this is in your relationships, in your career, with your health, and so on.

Life is about cycles within cycles, and in this book you have also been shown how to work out your Personal

Month, Personal Week and Personal Day Numbers too. However, these are lesser cycles within your overall yearly cycles and although they certainly do influence you, they are not as strong as your Personal Year Numbers. However, their lessons are the same, so by looking up each number in the Personal Year section, you will also see your potential for that month, week or day too.

You may identify with some of the qualities or experiences associated with each number cycle 1 to 9, and the lessons they hold. However, each number contains its potential, and therefore you may not experience everything within that Personal Year cycle. This may be for many reasons. Perhaps you are still working strongly with the previous or consecutive number cycle, or a little of both of these together. That is, if you are influenced by a 7 Personal Year and you do not identify with its qualities perhaps it is because the number 6 or number 8 is influencing you more strongly at that time. However, in essence the actual Personal Year cycle you are in carries the strongest influence over your life. You may also interpret each Personal Year cycle and adapt them to your life according to the sequence of numbers already in your numerology chart. So you may experience a 5 Personal Year, for example, differently to someone else. However, the basic lessons remain the same.

THE BASIC LESSONS OF EACH
NUMEROLOGICAL CYCLE

Year 1

During a 1 Personal Year cycle you are influenced by new beginnings, new direction and new starts. Perhaps during this cycle you rise to these qualities and change your life on some level, or in some way. You may experience a big move forward during this 1 cycle or may also feel a loss of direction too.

Year 2

This 2 Personal Year highlights balance and it is also associated with emotional balance too. During this cycle you may find yourself weighing up all the situations in your life in order to try to bring in this quality. Therefore situations which seem out of balance in your life may be brought to your attention during this 2 cycle.

Year 3

Expansion is one of the key qualities of this 3 Personal Year. You may also feel frustrated when life doesn't expand you in the direction you want during this 3 cycle. At other times if you find your life moving forward fast then you may draw yourself back to try to stop the flow.

Year 4

During this Personal Year 4 you are working to consolidate the previous 3 years of experiences (and of course all the other cycles previous to that). The 4 energy also highlights grounding and is testing you to be able to survive, even when life seems up in the air, as consolidating may mean you need to rearrange your life in some way.

Year 5

This 5 Personal Year highlights movement, and although life is constantly moving, during this cycle you may be more aware of changes in your life. Sometimes changes may seem very small but they may have an enormous impact in your life, and at other times you may feel fully able to cope with bigger changes during this 5 cycle.

Year 6

Wholeness is one of the major qualities highlighted in this 6 Personal Year. Wholeness means being aware that everyone is a part of one world, and also being aware of all the different aspects in yourself too. During this 6 cycle, even when you feel complete and whole you can always find more to learn about.

Year 7

The 7 year cycle is a motivating energy which helps you to synthesize all the lessons you have learned during your last 6 cycles, in order to *complete* with those issues and experiences in some way. Sometimes this period may be very productive and at other times you may feel a sense of loss on some level during this cycle.

Year 8

The number 8 brings in the quality of karma, or the law of what you give out you get back from others and from life. Therefore you may wonder why you may win the lottery during this cycle, or even find yourself in the most unusual situations. The 8 highlights the need to re-evaluate your life during this Personal Year.

Year 9

The number 9 brings in the quality of endings and new beginnings where you are ending one 9 year cycle and preparing for another new 9 year cycle. Therefore this may be a time for great transformation, which need not be dramatic, but perhaps simply means you acknowledge all that has gone before in the last 9 years.

Universal Years

In summing up this book's usefulness to you it is essential to mention that situations contained within your Personal Year Numbers are not guaranteed. This is because of the influence of the Universal Year Number which influences everyone. For example, in the year 2010, then 3 is the Universal Year Number (add $2 + 0 + 1 + 0 = 3$). These universal numbers influence world trends, like the economy, health trends, weather trends, and so on, which can bring changes into your life at any given time.

Your Numbers Up

Numbers keep teaching you and even when you think you know a lot about each number in your chart there is still more to learn. Indeed it is impossible to write a complete book which explains all the many, many different facets and qualities contained within each number 1 to 9 or how these numbers play their part in life. This is because each day numbers are evolving to give you more information about them. For example, if you take the language of vocabulary, even over the most recent times the dictionary has grown with the addition of many modern words which simply did not exist even fifty years ago.

This is the same with numerology: each generation places its own interpretation on to each number (or the numbers mirror back the inner process which each society is going through). This exciting aspect of numerology encourages you to apply observation to how numbers influence your life and also to use your intuition to allow the numbers to speak to you.

Numerology is fascinating, and if you find yourself wanting more, then there are wonderful books to buy, workshops to attend, and professional training. And of course you can even develop your own kind of numerology by writing down what you think each number means too. Numerology is a wonderful gift which can teach you more about yourself and this rich life on earth.

CONTACTS

For numerology readings, workshops and professional training, visit the website for Association Internationale de Numerologues (AIN) and The Connaissance School of Numerology:

www.numerology.org.uk.

You can also send a stamped addressed envelope or international reply coupon to:

AIN
8 Melbourne Street
Royston
SG8 7BZ
UK